SERIOUS SURVIVAL STRATEGIES

FOR VICTORY

SERIOUS SURVIVAL STRATEGIES

FOR VICTORY

BY
PASTOR ROD PARSLEY

RESULTS

PUBLISHING

Columbus, Ohio

TABLE OF CONTENTS

INTRODUCTION

"This know also, that in the last days perilous times shall come. For men shall be lovers of their own selves, covetous, boasters, proud, blasphemers, disobedient to parents, unthankful, unholy, Without natural affection, trucebreakers, false accusers, incontinent, fierce, despisers of those that are good, Traitors, heady, highminded, lovers of pleasures more than lovers of God; Having a form of godliness, but denying the power thereof: from such turn away. For of this sort are they which creep into houses, and lead captive silly women laden with sins, led away with divers lusts, Ever learning, and never able to come to the knowledge of the truth" (2 Timothy 3:1-7).

A PROPHETIC CALL TO REALITY

I have a prophetic word for you: **troubled times are upon us!** Many read the above passage in 2 Timothy 3 and say, "Well, Pastor Rod, times have always been perilous. What makes this time in spiritual history any different?"

NEVER BEFORE in the history of man has such potential existed for our own destruction. Hydrogen bombs are so powerful that they require an atomic bomb to detonate them!

Scientists claim that if a large hydrogen bomb ever exploded in our earth's atmosphere, the shocks could cause an imbalance which would bring civilization, as we know it, to a standstill.

Times have always been perilous, but this is THE PERILOUS TIME!

Men and women *"without natural affection"* are engaging in homosexual and lesbian activity despite the endtime generation's plague of AIDS — a killer that man cannot stop. AIDS-infected people who are *"lovers of pleasure"* continue to have sex at any cost with multiple partners ... without ever informing them about their HIV infection. These *"lovers of their own selves"* want self-gratification in sex — even if it means DEATH to their partners!

We have never seen a time like this!

The secular media has become open *"despisers of those that are good,"* constantly showing Christianity in a negative light and refusing to depict any Christian as intelligent, warm, considerate, or loving.

America was founded on a STRONG BELIEF in the guiding hand of God, yet that belief is being pushed aside by those who have a religion of self-interest and self-indulgence. The message of the last decade in America has been to "do our own thing" and "just be happy," yet we suddenly wake up to a nation where prayer is yanked out of schools, nativity scenes are forbidden in our parks, and songs about Jesus cannot be sung at any public school Christmas celebration!

America is becoming a moral wasteland, where half of all marriages end in divorce — where men and women who have become *"lovers of their own selves"* are willing to sacrifice their marriage covenants on the altar of self-indulgent pleasure.

Our country is exploding with "growth groups" that put you "in touch" with the god-you ... not God, but the YOU who is supposedly a god. They talk about inner-strength, inner self-fulfillment, and hundreds of other lofty-sounding terms. The stark reality is they do not know God, and only portray a *"form of godliness."*

Friend, we have never seen a day like today!

How can your marriage stay strong if you watch one adulterous affair after another on TV soap operas?

How can your husband continue to look good to you when he fails to meet the youthful, sexy appearance of the young doctor on the latest daytime drama?

Clearly, TV is "creeping into homes," and presenting situations to take men and women captive *"with divers lusts."* The writers of these programs never, EVER portray any negative moral results from these sinful liaisons.

Our young children, just reaching the age of puberty, are "educated" on how to use condoms, but NEVER counseled about the emotional or moral traumas that can result from a sexual relationship at an early age. These same children are then "counseled" on how to secure an abortion without parental permission, yet they cannot go to the school nurse and get an aspirin without a note from their parents!

We are living in a uniquely evil day!

These are the final moments of endtime spiritual history!

America has stopped making any moral sense!

We have the most modern technological advances to <u>save lives</u> in the history of the universe, YET ... one unborn child is aborted for every 21 seconds that tick on the clock.

We have the most advanced printing presses and computer typesetting ever available to publish the Word of God, YET ... billions of dollars are spent publishing child pornography. 300,000 children have been subjected to reported sexual exploitation ... in the last 18 months!

We have Christian libraries and bookstores filled with information about our Savior, YET ... there are over 100,000 practicing witches in the United States.

We are *"ever learning, and never able to come to the knowledge of the truth."*

We are *"ever learning, and never able to come to the knowledge of the truth."*

Man has never seen a time like today.

This book is intended to awaken and encourage you to a prophetic reality ... it is a word in season to them that are weary (Isaiah 50:4). Friend, there is hope for you beyond the scope of human limitation!

If you look to America for hope, you will find a moral wasteland of empty promises and vanishing dreams.

America can no longer cope with exploding catastrophes in the cities and in the nation.

The boiling, brewing caldron of racial hatred explodes time and time again in incidents like the police beating of Rodney King in Los Angeles and the subsequent riots.

The Federal deficit of $4.1 trillion, the business deficit of $3 trillion, and the individual debt of $4 trillion have left our country economically ravaged, unable to function fiscally or compete effectively with other major nations. These deficits reflect the GREED that infects every fiber of our nation, the "I want it all" mentality that so dominated life in the decade of the eighties.

We live in a nation where a few owls are suddenly more important than the welfare of tens of thousands of families, and where a few whales are more valuable than millions of babies.

It is time for us to refuse to allow our future to be dominated or dictated to by the flesh, according to human limitations.

It is time for us to lift your eyes beyond the seen into the unseen; we must see what cannot be seen, and hear what cannot be heard.

Paul said, *"While we look not at the things which are seen, but at the things which are not seen: for the things which are seen are temporal; but the things which are not seen are eternal"* (2 Corinthians 4:18).

This is a paradox. How do we look at something that cannot be seen?

We must know the answer to survive in America's endtime wasteland.

We need biblical "Survival Strategies" to face temptation, to conquer cancer, to cast off the attacks of anti-Christians, to survive the financial failures all around us.

We must know how to survive the perils of perilous times.

Paul said, *"I know both how to be abased, and I know how to abound: every where and in all things I am instructed both to be full and to be hungry, both to abound and to suffer need. I can do all things through Christ which strengtheneth me"* (Philippians 4:12,13).

In this passage, Paul was declaring, "I have been in the perils of the deep, in the perils of my countrymen, and in the perils of affliction; I have been in the middle of the desert; I have been left for dead! But I have learned how to survive the perils of perilous times."

This is NOT a Popular Message!

I know you would rather read a message that tells you things are going to get better, but the Bible tells us ... IT IS NOT GOING TO GET BETTER, IT IS GOING TO GET WORSE!

But God is here to protect and nurture and love you in the midst of the perilous times.

There is hope for your discouragement!

Even Elijah became discouraged.

"But he himself went a day's journey into the wilderness, and came and sat down under a juniper tree: and he requested for himself that he might die; and said, It is enough; now, O Lord, take away my life; for I am not better than my fathers" (1 Kings 19:4).

Elijah had just come through the greatest victory of his ministry.

Always remember this: the greatest conflict will come on the heels of the greatest victory. The peril of the mountain top is when you are there you have the delusion that you are always going to be there.

Elijah was a man of God, and God sent His angel to minister to him.

"And as he lay and slept under a juniper tree, behold, then an angel touched him, and said

unto him, Arise and eat. And he looked, and, behold, there was a cake baken on the coals, and a cruse of water at his head. And he did eat and drink, and laid him down again" (1 Kings 19:5,6).

The Kingdom of God is not all mountain tops!

There are going to be some valleys.

The same God who ministered to Elijah is standing ready to meet your every need!

Every now and then there is a cup of sorrow to drink. When sorrow does come into your life — and it will — do not take the popular and immature stance running around in many Christian circles that says, "Anything that is discomforting to my flesh comes from the devil."

Nonsense!

Go beyond that limited teaching to the point where you realize that though it may have come from the devil, you are walking a consecrated life, you are walking the highway of holiness (Isaiah 35:8), your steps are ordered of the Lord (Psalm 37:23). Whatever you step into may not have come from the Lord, but it was allowed by your Father ... and if you will allow it, it will produce Christlikeness in you.

God wants you like Jesus.

Paul was a man who knew how to survive the perils of perilous times, a man who knew that there was hope beyond the scope of humanity for him and for everyone that he came in contact with.

Get beyond the mentality that "all I have to do is get up in the morning and rebuke the devil."

There is something you need to do <u>before</u> you rebuke the devil.

James 4:7 does not simply say, *"Resist the devil, and he will flee from you."* It says, *"Submit yourselves therefore to God. Resist the devil, and he will flee from you."*

Submitting comes first.

Submitting says, "I yield my control to God. I will no longer take the Word of God and try to get my own way with it."

In Genesis 32:24-31, Jacob saw God face to face. He was then a marked man — he walked differently, and all could see. I want to be like Jacob. I want people to see that I have been in the mountain with God, in contact with the great I AM!

"Well, Pastor Rod," you say, "I can't believe God would let this peril come into my life."

Jesus is looking for people who will stand up for Him, even when a cup of sorrow comes their way.

17

How much could you let go out of your life and you not let go of God?

This planet is a mess.

America is cursed.

You cannot get a rose without a thorn.

If you think you are going to tiptoe through the tulips and never experience a cup of sorrow, or never experience a perilous time, or never feel like the heavens are brass ... then you have made a serious, tragic mistake!

God is shaking the world!

People are walking through the fiery furnace.

Do you know what you have to hold onto to survive the perils of perilous times?

Him!

When you do not know where to turn, the only way to turn is up.

When you do not know what to do, the first thing to do is pray.

"Brethren, I count not myself to have apprehended: but this one thing I do, forgetting those things which are behind, and reaching forth unto those things which are before, I press toward the mark for the prize of the high calling of God in Christ Jesus" (Philippians 3:13,14).

In that passage, Paul was telling the Philippians, "I'm fastening my eyes on Christ.

If you want to follow anything, follow the way I'm following Him. Do not follow me, but follow my following. Follow the way that I trust in Him when I'm walking through the fire. Follow the way I reach out for a hand bigger than my hand. Follow my following."

Some of you are facing the greatest trials and conflicts of your life — and you are not alone.

God is shaking this world.

"Whose voice then shook the earth: but now he hath promised, saying, Yet once more I shake not the earth only, but also heaven. And this word, Yet once more, signifieth the removing of those things that are shaken, as of things that are made, that those things which cannot be shaken may remain" (Hebrews 12:26,27).

There are people right now who are losing their careers for no other reason than they are Christians!

We must learn how to survive!

If a bill that has been introduced in Congress passes, homosexuality will be a constitutionally protected right. In many states, there are now laws which bind even churches to hiring homosexuals to work on their staffs, if they are qualified for the job. Morals cannot be a consideration.

We must learn how to survive!

In Russia, the Holy Bible can be taught in the classrooms; but in America, a public school teacher cannot even put a copy of the Ten Commandments up in the classroom.

We must learn how to survive!

Women's rights groups can freely demonstrate in public forums without criticisms; but when Christians mobilize, we are accused by the media of trying to "force" our will on others. We must learn how to survive!

It is only in our surviving that the victory that is beyond the scope of humanity is proven to a skeptical world.

"But ye are come unto mount Sion, and unto the city of the living God, the heavenly Jerusalem, and to an innumerable company of angels," (Hebrews 12:22).

That verse tells us we have come into the realm of the spirit, which lies beyond the horizon of human perception; the only way for you to access that realm is in the Spirit.

That is how Paul, who learned to survive the perils of perilous times, found himself imprisoned in the sewage systems of Rome, and yet he said, *"Blessed be the God and Father of our Lord Jesus Christ, who hath blessed us with all spiritual blessings in heavenly places in Christ:" (Ephesians 1:3).*

He was not sitting in his mansion with a multitude of servants, eating fruit on stems and drinking mineral water.

He was in prison!

But Paul said, "God hath raised me up."

To survive the perils of perilous times, you have to learn that your natural circumstances do not dictate your spiritual altitude. Your body can be in the natural — in the flatlands with the ducks — while your spirit is soaring across the snowcapped peaks of mighty mountains with the eagle nature of the Spirit of God!

"To the general assembly of the church of the firstborn, which are written in heaven, and to God the Judge of all, and to the spirits of just men made perfect, and to Jesus the mediator of the new covenant, and of the blood of sprinkling, that speaketh better things than that of Abel. See that ye refuse not him that speaketh. For if they escaped not who refused him that spake on earth, much more shall not we escape, if we turn away from him that speaketh from heaven: Whose voice then shook the earth: but now he hath promised, saying, Yet once more I shake not the earth only, but also heaven. And this word, Yet once more, signifieth the removing of things that are shaken, as of the things that are made, that those things which cannot be shaken may remain" (Hebrews 12:23-27).

There are about to be some changes.

21

Paul declared, "We are part of this thing we call the natural realm; and the only thing that is going to survive this shaking is not what is born of the flesh, and not what is founded on flesh, but rather, that which is born of the Spirit."

You are born of the Spirit of God; you are not just a natural man.

When His Son lay wrapped in grave clothes in the borrowed tomb of Joseph of Arimathaea, and while the demon hordes of hell howled and cackled in the bowels of perdition, God did not hang His head. And when hell had done its worst to the best that heaven had to offer, God raised Him from the dead, proving and loudly proclaiming that there is hope beyond the confines of mortality!

Stand on the sandy shore and look out as far as your eye can see, and see that place where heaven kisses earth and the sea caresses the glory of the heavens.

Look as far as you can see on that same sandy beach, and suddenly, you will see something pop up over the edge of what you can see with your natural eye.

Jesus was the seed of David according to the flesh, but just over the horizon, just beyond what could be seen with human eyes, was the miraculous resurrection from the dead!

He surfaced beyond the border of mortal man's domain when He kicked the end out of the grave and resurrected with power, triumphing over death, hell, and the grave.

There is hope for you beyond the scope of human limitation, but you are not going to experience it just looking in the natural all the time and being dictated to by your feelings.

"Well," you say, "it's just so gloomy today."

So what?

There is hope beyond the scope of human limitation living on the inside of you! Get ready.

Things will be shaken.

Some will be required to walk through the lonesome valley.

Jesus went through the trial of perilous times; He went into the grave, but He came out victorious on the other side.

Seek That Which Endures

The things you see are temporal, subject to change.

There are only three things that endure.

First, the graces of God.

"And now abideth faith, hope, charity, these three; but the greatest of these is charity" (1 Corinthians 13:13).

Faith, hope and charity will endure and will sustain you through the perils of perilous times.

Second, the unseen things of the spirit realm endure (2 Corinthians 4:18). That is the reason the Word endures."

Heaven and earth shall pass away, but my words shall not pass away" (Matthew 24:35).

And third, His kingdom endures.

"Wherefore we receiving a kingdom which cannot be moved, let us have grace, whereby we may serve God acceptably with reverence and godly fear" (Hebrews 12:28).

You are part of a kingdom which cannot be shaken, cannot be removed, and cannot fall apart; it is going to endure!

You are going to be there when the new Jerusalem, 1,500 miles square, comes down out of the very being of God; you get to live there!

Here is an endtime prophecy: Do not worry about the economy. You can survive if every bank on this planet blows up.

People start to panic if the savings and loans begin to crash.

You can survive when there are no more savings and loans!

Yes, the economy is falling apart, but your finances can remain strong!

Yes, sorrowfully there are thousands with AIDS, but it shall not come nigh thee.

Lift up your eyes.

Quit looking at what you can see, and look at what you cannot see. Angels are walking all around you; the fiery hosts of heaven are surrounding you in everything you do.

Look!

See that blood covering you?

"Forasmuch then as the children are partakers of flesh and blood, he also himself likewise took part of the same; that through death he might destroy him that had the power of death, that is, the devil;" (Hebrews 2:14).

His blood covers you.

You are blood-bought into a supernatural Kingdom that cannot be moved. The only time you have to fear anything is when you step outside that Kingdom.

The devil is a thief; he does not have to be strong. All he has to do is catch you "not at home" in the realm of the spirit.

Read This Book Prayerfully

As you prayerfully read these essential keys to spiritual survival, remember, *"God is our refuge and strength, a very present help in trouble. Therefore will not we fear though the earth be removed, and though the mountains be carried into the midst of the sea; Though the waters thereof roar and be troubled, though the*

mountains shake with the swelling thereof.
Selah" (Psalm 46:1-3).

Right now, you may feel like your world is falling apart.

Remember Psalm 46.

"Selah" means be still, settle down, take a minute and relax.

God will preserve you in the midst of trouble.

Many Christians want to stick their heads in the sand and pretend everything in life is just beautiful.

How can life be beautiful when 4,500 babies a day are being stripped out of the wombs of their mothers?

How can life be beautiful when the justice system allows police officers to beat a man 70 times?

How can life be beautiful when lesbianism and homosexuality are portrayed as "normal" lifestyles?

Something is wrong.

Preachers are scorned; churches are dead and cold. There is a seeming dearth of the prophetic Word of God in the earth.

Things do not look good.

But God says, in the midst of perilous times, "Selah."

"Sit down a minute; relax. See the whole picture."

Psalm 46 continues:

"There is a river, the streams whereof shall make glad the city of God, the holy place of the tabernacles of the most High. God is in the midst of her; she shall not be moved: God shall help her, and that right early" (Psalm 46:4,5).

There is a river of God which shall make you glad, even in the midst of perilous circumstances.

This book will show you how to swim in that river!

In the last days, God promises to pour out His Spirit on all flesh.

"And it shall come to pass in the last days, saith God, I will pour out of my Spirit upon all flesh: and your sons and your daughters shall prophesy, and your young men shall see visions, and your old men shall dream dreams: And on my servants and my handmaidens I will pour out in those days of my Spirit; and they shall prophesy: And I will shew wonders in heaven above, and signs in the earth beneath; blood, and fire, and vapour of smoke" (Acts 2:17-19).

God is going to turn up the heat, but you will be swimming in the living water of the Holy Spirit!

"Be glad then, ye children of Zion, and rejoice in the Lord your God: for he hath given you the former rain moderately, and he will cause to come down for you the rain, the former rain, and the latter rain in the first month. And the floors shall be full of wheat, and the vats shall overflow with wine and oil" (Joel 2:23-24).

You will be washed in the former rain and the latter rain all together in one month!

There is a Holy Spirit flood coming; get ready to jump in!

While the banks of the world are failing, get ready, because you house will overflow with oil and be full with wheat!

Jump in the river of the precious Holy Ghost.

Feed Your Spirit Man

So many Christians appear strong and healthy on the outside, but on the inside they are little emaciated characters, elbows bigger than arms, knees sticking out bigger than thighs, eyes sunk back in their heads, barely able to move.

Their spirits are weak and tired.

Why?

Because they are not feeding the spirit man.

Many claim that they want to be "spiritual giants," but spend all their time feeding the natural man.

28

In these perilous times, your natural man cannot cope with the circumstances. You will feel like pulling your hair out by the roots, and your little trembling hand will reach out for a hand bigger than yours — but there will be no hand to grab, no place to turn.

At that needy moment, you will turn to your spirit and ask your spirit to respond as though you have been feeding him three times a day, when you barely feed him three times a week!

The Bible says, *"For which cause we faint not; but though our outward man perish, yet the inward man is <u>renewed day by day</u>" (2 Corinthians 4:16, my emphasis).*

Do you want to know how to successfully navigate the perils of perilous times?

Read and put into ACTION the twenty survival strategies contained in this book.

The Holy Ghost will safely navigate you down a river of peace while others all around you are drowning.

When your husband walks in and says, "I do not happen to like your looks anymore. I'm leaving you," God has a river of living water for you.

When the doctor looks at you and says "You have to die; you cannot live with this cancer," there are streams of living water that run straight from the city of God and the tabernacles of the Most High to you.

God shall come to you as the rain, the former rain, and the latter rain — all in the same month!

"He that believeth on me, as the scripture hath said, out of his belly shall flow rivers of living water" (John 7:38).

There is a river flowing out of your innermost being; you are a spirit man.

When you are going through the perils of perilous times, your spirit man can grasp hold of the anchor of the Word of the Almighty and say, "This is it. I do not care what it looks like, sounds like, smells like, or feels like. I can see beyond the scope of human limitation, and there is hope beyond that scope."

If you are going to survive, you need to stir up your spirit and grasp hold of this Word.

I do not care what you are facing as you read this book, or what you will face tomorrow. If you will apply the spiritual principles contained in these "Survival Strategies," you will be victorious.

Here are the facts

One: Perilous times are coming.
Two: You are a spirit man.

If you are going to survive the perils of perilous times and have hope beyond the scope of human limitation, you are going to have to realize you are a spirit man.

Get stirred up in your spirit.

Pray in the Holy Ghost.

Become intimately acquainted with the Spirit of the Living God, and be led by His Spirit. The spiritually dead are led by their head. Start to be led by your spirit.

Three: God's Word is infallible.

The Word is the oak of God planted in the forest of eternity, entwining its roots around the Rock of Ages. Take hold of God's Word. Though heaven and earth pass away, though the world be on fire, you will stand and watch it burn. You will successfully navigate the trials of perilous times.

As you recognize these three facts, and begin to apply these "Survival Strategies" in your life, your victory, even during these unprecedented perilous times, is assured.

Be Born Again — to the Bone

A Queen's Faith

John Townsend wrote a letter to Queen Victoria, urging her to read John 3:16 and Romans 10:9,10 so she might know that the eternal life promised in the Bible is sure both for the present and the future.

About two weeks later, Mr. Townsend received the following reply:

"Your letter of recent date received, and in reply I would state that I have carefully and prayerfully read the portions of Scripture referred to. I believe in the finished work of Christ for me, and trust by God's grace to meet you in that Home of which He said, 'I go to prepare a place for you.'"

— (signed) Queen Victoria

"Therefore if any man be in Christ, he is a new creature: old things are passed away; behold, all things are become new" (2 Corinthians 5:17).

"If you are going to survive the onslaught of hell in the last days, make sure you are born again to the bone."
                                        -Pastor Rod Parsley

The first key to survival is salvation!

My friend, you need to be born again!

2 Corinthians 5:17 says, *"If any man be in Christ, he is a new creature: old things are passed away; behold, all things are become new."*

If you are going to survive the onslaught of hell in these last days, make sure you are born again to the bone.

There is salvation in no other name except the name of Jesus Christ of Nazareth.

There is no salvation in a Shinto shrine or a Buddhist temple.

You can lick a crystal until your tongue falls out, and it will not get you into the gates of the Heavenly City.

There is no salvation in a New Age god.

There is only one way to obtain salvation, and that is trusting in the blood-stained cross of Jesus Christ!

"Wherefore God also hath highly exalted him, and given him a name which is above every name: That at the name of Jesus every knee should bow, of things in heaven, and things in earth, and things under the earth; And that every

tongue should confess that Jesus Christ is Lord, to the glory of God the Father" (Philippians 2:9-11).

Salvation is not just walking down an aisle or signing a piece of paper or going to a neighborhood church.

You will never get to heaven just by being a nice person.

You will never get to heaven just by paying your taxes, or by being an upstanding person in the community.

There is only one way to heaven!

Jesus said, *"I am the way, the truth, and the life: no man cometh unto the Father, but by me" (John 14:6).*

Nicodemus, a ruler of the Jews, came to Jesus seeking God. Jesus told him, *"Verily, verily, I say unto thee, Except a man be born again, he cannot see the Kingdom of God" (John 3:3).*

I did not say that, Jesus did!

Alive in Christ

C.M. Ward said:

"Anything alive must have an appetite.
Anything alive must have discharge.
Anything alive must have growth.
Anything alive must have reproduction."

If you are "alive" through Christ Jesus, if you are a new man through the "born-again" salvation experience, then these four areas will manifest themselves in your life.

You will have an appetite to know all that you can know about the nature of God.

"Even the Spirit of truth; whom the world cannot receive, because it seeth him not, neither knoweth him: but ye know him; for he dwelleth with you, and shall be in you" (John 14:17).

You will desire to discharge, to put aside all the things that excite the world but are not profitable to God.

"He that loveth his life shall lose it; and he that hateth his life in this world shall keep it unto life eternal" (John 12:25).

You will have the desire to grow each day in those things which bring you closer to the nature of Jesus Christ.

"But put ye on the Lord Jesus Christ, and make not provision for the flesh, to fulfil the lusts thereof" (Romans 13:14).

You will manifest reproduction through your evangelistic calling to bring your neighbors and friends to the Lord, to become sons of God.

"But as many as received him, to them gave he power to become the sons of God, even to them that believe on his name" (John 1:12).

When you receive salvation, your appetites and your allegiances change.

Satan Hates His Own Children

Do not play around with your salvation.

You are either a child of the devil or a child of God; and you should know the devil hates his own kids. He will use you, abuse you, and destroy you as long as you play around in his kingdom.

"The thief cometh not, but for to steal, and to kill, and to destroy" (John 10:10).

The devil promises a rainbow, but delivers rain.

He promises the world, but delivers hell.

He is a liar, and the father of lies.

"Ye are of your father the devil, and the lusts of your father ye will do. He was a murderer from the beginning, and abode not in the truth, because there is no truth in him. When he speaketh a lie, he speaketh of his own: for he is a liar, and the father of it" (John 8:44).

Salvation Means "Whole In God"

Jesus' crucifixion and resurrection purchased salvation for us. The word that is translated as "salvation" has a much broader meaning than many people think. That word is "sozo" — to deliver, protect, heal, make whole, preserve, and do well by.

We need to get as close to God as we can in the endtime hour of spiritual history. We must allow the full manifestation of salvation in every area of our life.

As Satan's attack intensifies, the child of God needs to know how to pray, and then do it.

"He shall call upon me, and I will answer him: I will be with him in trouble; I will deliver him, and honour him" (Psalm 91:15).

The child of God needs to know how to give, and then do it.

"Give, and it shall be given unto you; good measure, pressed down, and shaken together, and running over, shall men give into your bosom. For with the same measure that ye mete withal it shall be measured to you again" (Luke 6:38).

The child of God needs to know how to fast, and then do it.

"And she was a widow of about fourscore and four years, which departed not from the temple, but served God with fastings and prayers night and day" (Luke 2:37).

The child of God needs to know how to live right, and then needs do it.

"Neither yield ye your members as instruments of unrighteousness unto sin; but yield yourselves unto God, as those that are alive from the dead, and your members as instruments of righteousness unto God" (Romans 6:13).

To spiritually survive, it is vital for you to have an up-to-date relationship with the King of Kings and the Lord of Lords ... because the devil hates everything about you.

He despises you, and he will bring all hell to bear on your life to destroy you.

"Be sober, be vigilant; because your adversary the devil, as a roaring lion, walketh about, seeking whom he may devour" (1 Peter 5:8).

Your only hope is to run out of the darkness and run into the light — to be born again by the Spirit of God — and get translated out of the kingdom of darkness and into the Kingdom of Light.

"Through the tender mercy of our God; whereby the dayspring from on high hath visited us, To give light to them that sit in darkness and in the shadow of death, to guide our feet into the way of peace" (Luke 1:78,79).

Desperate times demand desperate action

We are living in the last days.

If you do not think the devil is angry, you are wrong. He has zeroed his sights in on the church. The church is detestable in his sight; he hates it. Satan hates every person who names the name of Christ, and he especially hates the blood-bought, Holy Ghost-filled crowd that is not backing up to him.

This is not the time to fold your hands, to let your head hang down, to be sad, or to roll your eyes like a dying calf and be religious.

This is the time that the earth should break forth into praise, that the mountains and the hills should break forth into singing!

Everyone who names the name of Christ must release the power that is resident on the inside of them!

You may say, "That is too emotional, Pastor Rod. I can just stand here quietly and praise the Lord."

If you do, you can watch the devil steal your kids, send your business rocking and reeling into bankruptcy, or manifest some fatal cancer or other disease upon you.

You are the decision-maker.

Desperate times demand desperate action.

The devil has already devised a plan for your tomorrow, so thwart his plan today. With everything that is in you praise Him for your salvation that allows you to walk victorious through these perilous times.

"If any man speak, let him speak as the oracles of God; if any man minister, let him do it as of the ability which God giveth: that God in all things may be glorified through Jesus Christ, to whom be praise and dominion for ever and ever. Amen" (1 Peter 4:11).

> *"If we can receive a revelation of who Jesus is, we can take our place in the kingdom, and the gates of hell will not prevail against us."*
> *- Pastor Rod Parsley*

This is spiritual war, and we need to realize it.

The first century church had to pray Simon Peter out of trouble time and time again because Satan had targeted him as a key man to attack.

When Herod sent forth his soldiers to persecute certain men in the church, one of those he particularly wanted to persecute was Peter — because Peter knew who Jesus was, and was considered a spiritual field general (Acts 12:1-3).

Jesus asked Peter, *"But whom say ye that I am?" (Matthew 16:15).*

Without a moment's hesitation, up out of the belly of that great fisherman came the words, *"Thou art the Christ, the Son of the living God" (Matthew 16:16).*

Jesus said, *"Blessed art thou, Simon Barjona: for flesh and blood hath not revealed it unto thee, but my Father which is in heaven ... and upon this rock [of revelation] I will build my church; and the gates of hell shall not prevail against it" (Matthew 16:17,18).*

Because Peter knew who God was, and because God had a purpose for Peter, the enemy especially targeted him as a source of attack.

Do you ever wonder why the same devil who attacked Peter is always picking on you?

Because you know too much!

He is not worried about the so-and-so church that sings the first, second, and last verse of some dried-up old song in an ancient hymnal.

He is not worried if you listen to some six-foot icicle stand up in the pulpit to moan and groan and hurriedly deliver a twenty minute sermonette so you can get down to the dinette and have a cigarette.

Satan is only worried about people who know the nature of Jesus, and are willing to serve Him as generals in God's endtime army.

He is only worried about those who are serious about making it all the way to the heavenly city.

The enemy is only worried about those who are serious about depopulating the corridors of hell and increasing the population of heaven.

Take your place in God's army and in the Kingdom of God ... where the gates of hell will not prevail against you in any manner, shape or form (Matthew 16:18).

You need to realize that spiritual warfare is not a game, and that the devil is not some innocent puppy. He is the master deceiver, thief, murderer, and the force behind all evil.

I am talking about the spirit that got in a man and made him calculate how to lure other young men into his apartment and drug them, and then take a knife and dismember them.

Satan will damn your soul to hell if you let him.

It is time to get serious about spiritual warfare and about the devil.

He is the gnawing of cancer, the dollar bill in the pocket of the abortion doctor, the blank stare in the face of the homeless.

He is the cold ache of arthritis, the limp of one crippled, the despair of poverty.

He is the desperate sob of a little girl alone in her bedroom, nursing a bruised cheek that has been slapped by her daddy.

He is the author of fear and the father of lies.

He is the panic of sirens, the overcrowding of county jails and federal penitentiaries; he is the source of arguing, insanity, slander, lying, cheating, stealing, heresy, and sedition.

He is the reality and the necessity of an eternal hell.

He is the driving impulse of every sexual perversion, of homosexuality, of lesbianism, and of all drug and alcohol addiction.

He is the blackness of midnight, the power of pagan religion, and the despair of funerals.

He is behind every rape, every incest. He is the perpetrator of prejudice and slavery.

He is the multiplied hideousness of Hitler and Hussein.

He is suicide, teen pregnancy, the occult, demonic possession, New Age deceit.

He is the backbiting of friends, the jagged edge of a tattered relationship.

He is the deceitfulness of earthly security. He is everything cruel, painful, fierce. He is the source of every plague, curse, and blight known to the human family.

He is the original instigator of separation between the Creator and His creation, yet we try to act and live like he is not even in our world!

To survive his attacks, you must realize that spiritual warfare is not a game, and that the devil is a real enemy, hell-bent on destroying you.

Understand right now that the devil is out to stop you, and determine to get serious about how to rebuke him and keep him from hindering your service to the Lord.

"Until you recognize you are lost without God, destined to spend eternity in hell without His rescuing help, you will never be truly saved."
- Pastor Rod Parsley

No one can touch you like Jesus. If you want to be touched and changed right now, God knows your heart.

The first step to experiencing a personal relationship with Jesus — to receiving Him — is repenting of your sin.

Sin separates us from God. Until you recognize you are lost without God, destined to spend eternity in hell without His rescuing help, you will never be truly saved. You are empty inside; you have no life.

Open your heart and get ready right now to receive the outpouring of the priceless Lamb of God. If you want salvation and Jesus Christ to be part of your life, say this simple prayer out loud right now:

"Heavenly Father, I come to you as a sinner, born under sin's curse, a child of darkness and of rebellion. I recognize who I am and what I need. I don't need help; I need salvation. I don't just need to be touched; I need to be recreated.

"Lord Jesus Christ, you are the Son of the Living God. Your blood paid the price for my sin. I ask you now to become my Savior. I receive you as my Savior. I take you now as my

Redeemer to give me new life, to crush sin's curse, and to make me a new creation.

"Satan, I renounce you. You are not my god. I will not serve you. Go from me now!

"Lord Jesus Christ, I accept you, believe you, and confess you openly as my personal Savior. Thank you for the price you paid. From this day forward, I intend to serve you as you show me how. Thank you, Lord Jesus."

Welcome to the family of God!

You have taken the first step in mastering your "Survival Strategies."

I rejoice with you that you have had the honesty of heart to recognize your need to receive Jesus as personal Savior in your life! Through the coming days, weeks, months, and years, I know God will affirm your salvation and confirm the prayer you have just prayed.

Now that you are one of God's children, you have a new hope! Every situation you face, every circumstance that comes into your life can be victoriously defeated in the name of Jesus.

Become Bold in the Holy Ghost

Our Aim in Life

The Kurku, a hill tribe in India of some 98,000 people, have as their supreme desire and objective in life to be filled with demons. When filled, they believe, their lives will be immune to attack or harm from the evil forces. Oh yes, they believe in God, a good spirit, who created the world and created them. But he does them no harm, so they worship the evil spirits.

But what would happen if 98,000 of God's people in this land had as their supreme aim in life to be filled with the Holy Spirit? The Church of Christ would awaken, and before very long such a veritable stream of missionaries would be going forth that such poor souls as the demon worshipers of India might hear of our Savior.

- Student Foreign Missions Fellowship

"And when the day of Pentecost was fully come, they were all with one accord in one place. And suddenly there came a sound from heaven

as of a rushing mighty wind, and it filled all the house where they were sitting. And there appeared unto them cloven tongues like as of fire, and it sat upon each of them. And they were all filled with the Holy Ghost, and began to speak with other tongues, as the Spirit gave them utterance" (Acts 2:1-4).

"It is time to take the Holy Ghost plunge, to get baptized in the Holy Ghost, to get bold in God."

- Pastor Rod Parsley

Receiving an Acts 2:1-4 experience of the baptism in the Holy Ghost is a vital step for spiritual survival. It is time to take the Holy Ghost plunge, to get baptized in the Holy Ghost, to get bold in God!

It is time to walk around in your house like a person on fire from your loins up and from your loins down. It is time to surrender to the moving of the Holy Ghost and to be empowered to withstand Satan's devices in your life.

It is time to put down your foot, push back your plate, look up to heaven, and say, "I am not going to eat the king's meat. I am going to be like Shadrach, Meschach, and Abednego. I am going to walk through the fiery furnace, but it is not going to touch me. I am going to swim through the flood, but it shall not overflow me. I am going to get baptized in the Holy Ghost."

When you are baptized in the Holy Ghost, you receive fire — power inside of you to conquer every circumstance in your life.

The Proof is Pursuit

The PROOF of your desire for the Holy Spirit in your life is PURSUIT! When talking to Brother Mike Murdock several months ago, I remarked to him, "I'd sure like to play the piano like you do."

"No, you don't," he immediately replied.

I was a bit hurt by his quick reply, and thinking maybe what I said was not quite clear, I repeated my statement.

Mike again replied, "No, you don't."

"Well," I said, a bit frustrated, "what are you talking about?"

"Are you taking lessons?" he asked.

"No."

"Then you are not pursuing what you claim to desire."

Mike was right. If you want something, then the next step is to pursue it.

The proof of desire is pursuit.

If you want to activate the power of the Holy Ghost in your life and operate in the POWER of the gifts of the Spirit, then pursue your desire!

When God desired spiritual sons, He sent His only Son, Jesus, down to earth in pursuit of lost souls! When Jesus landed on this earth, He did not just stand back and stare. He came down from heaven, took your sins into His own body, and crucified sickness, disease, and sin on

Calvary. Then, he rose from the dead, forever defeating the forces of darkness.

When He ascended to heaven, He gave you POWER to overcome on earth.

"But ye shall receive POWER, after that the Holy Ghost is come upon you: and ye shall be witnesses unto me both in Jerusalem, and in all Judaea, and in Samaria, and unto the uttermost part of the earth" (Acts 1:8).

You need Holy Ghost POWER to survive!

POWER to sanctify your tongue.

POWER to live as God instructs you to live.

POWER to cast out devils and speak in new tongues.

POWER to be a witness for Jesus.

POWER to overcome in the middle of a troubled world, in the midst of perilous times.

"That word, I say, ye know, which was published throughout all Judaea, and began from Galilee, after the baptism which John preached; How God anointed Jesus of Nazareth with the Holy Ghost and with POWER: who went about doing good, and healing all that were oppressed of the devil; for God was with him" (Acts 10:37,38).

Do you see it?

Even Jesus received baptism of the Holy Ghost and POWER!

You cannot fight the devil on your own. Receiving the baptism of the Holy Ghost is a fundamental step in your spiritual survival.

51

"You do not know what the devil has plotted against you tomorrow, so pray in the Holy Ghost today."

- Pastor Rod Parsley

Some people who profess to be baptized in the Holy Ghost do not even pray in other tongues five minutes a week.

The Bible says, *"For he that speaketh in an unknown tongue speaketh not unto men, but unto God: for no man understandeth him; howbeit in the spirit he speaketh mysteries" (1 Corinthians 14:2).*

You pray and speak mysteries. You do not know what you are saying, but God does! When you pray in tongues in Los Angeles, California, a lady dying of cancer in Kansas City, Missouri, suddenly takes a turn for the better.

Your prayer in tongues releases a mystery, a miracle.

If you do not know how to pray for your teenager who is on drugs and alcohol, pray in the Holy Ghost.

If you do not know how to pray for your marriage that is seemingly hopeless in the natural, pray in the Holy Ghost.

You do not know what the devil has plotted against you tomorrow, so pray in the Holy Ghost today. You do not know what the next financial catastrophe will be during these hard economic times, so pray in the Holy Ghost.

"For we know not what we should pray for as we ought: but the Spirit itself maketh intercession for us with groanings which cannot be uttered" (Romans 8:26).

Get bold about the baptism in the Holy Ghost.

It is time for you to walk in the Holy Spirit for your spiritual survival!

Speaking in tongues is an outward sign of an inward work. It tells the devil, "I am no longer dominated by my mind, my will, and my emotions. My tongue is yielded to the Holy Spirit, even though my mind is void of understanding."

Every time I get on an airplane, I do not know what to pray, so I pray in tongues. Whenever possible, I place my hands on the outside of the plane, and I pray in tongues. There may be an airplane leaving Los Angeles while I am leaving Atlanta, and the devil may have a plan for them to meet in the air.

But there is someone on the inside of me watching over that situation. God knows all about it.

When I begin to pray in the Holy Ghost, I release my God-given POWER, and operate in a survival strategy that moves the hand of God on my behalf.

"When you are praying in the Holy Ghost, you are praying mysteries. You are stopping demonic attacks. You are breaking through into the spirit realm."

- Pastor Rod Parsley

One Sunday as I stood in my pulpit, I looked at the camera and said, "I see a man sitting in a hotel room with a cocktail in your hand. You drove there in a white truck with a yellow stripe. You were in the church at one time, but you are not anymore. You are called to ministry. In the name of Jesus, put that cocktail down, and give your life to God."

Later, that man called our office and gave us his testimony. Every detail was precise, and he gave his life to Jesus as a result of the words I spoke!

God had to have that television tape ready at the right time.

He had to have that service aired on television at exactly the right moment.

He had to stop that man's truck at enough traffic lights to make sure he was in that hotel when the program hit the air in his city.

Do you understand the scope of what God is doing?

Praying in the Holy Ghost is survival strategy. Why?

Praying in the Holy Ghost is survival strategy. Why?

When we pray in the Holy Ghost, we are praying mysteries, we are stopping demonic attacks, we are getting through into the spirit realm. We are gathering the angelic hosts around us; we are putting on our armor; we are ready for battle.

"The steps of a good man are ordered by the Lord" (Psalm 37:23).

We pick up our feet, He puts them down.

Stay prayed up, and God will be able to use you to invade enemy-held territory and bring a mighty deliverance to someone in need. Become personally, intimately acquainted with the third person of the Trinity, in whose dispensation we are currently living!

Learn how to flow freely in the Holy Ghost.

"As many as are led by the Spirit of God, they are the sons of God" (Romans 8:14).

I used to think we were automatically led by the Spirit of God because we are the sons of God. In actuality, it is the leading of the Holy Spirit that produces true sonship.

There are two Greek words for the word "sons." One is "teknon," one is "huios." "Teknon" means you are a son by right of birth. "Huios" means you are a son because you have

"Huios" is the word used in Romans 8:14. It does not mean you are a "son" just because you were born again. There are many people who are born again who do not have this kind of relationship. They are not led by the Spirit of God; they are led by their senses — by what they reason in their mind is right or wrong.

To be led by the Spirit of God, you must know Him — and knowing Him begins with prayer.

The apostle Paul stressed the importance of praying in tongues. *"What is it then? I will pray with the spirit, and I will pray with the understanding also" (1 Corinthians 14:15).* He went on to say, *"I thank my God, I speak with tongues more than ye all" (v.18).*

STRATEGY THREE

Never Lose Sight of Eternity

"Having been called to preach the gospel, God forbid that I stoop to be king."
- C.H. Spurgeon

"And while they looked steadfastly toward heaven as he went up, behold, two men stood by them in white apparel; Which also said, Ye men of Galilee, why stand ye gazing up into heaven? this same Jesus, which is taken up from you into heaven, shall so come in like manner as ye have seen him go into heaven" (Acts 1:10,11).

"When you feel like giving up, keep eternity in front of you, and realize you have come too far to turn back now."
                                        - Pastor Rod Parsley

Do you want to survive?

Never lose sight of eternity.

Have a heaven and a hell consciousness; have an eternity consciousness. When you see loved ones you know are not in the ark of safety, let your first thought be a vision of them plunging into eternity in hell.

Keep heaven ever before you. It is a real place — the place where Jesus now dwells. Heaven is mentioned 559 times in the Bible.

"Which he wrought in Christ, when he raised him from the dead, and set him at his own right hand in the heavenly places, Far above all principality, and power, and might, and dominion, and every name that is named, not only in this world, but also in that which is to come" (Ephesians 1:20,21).

Reject the lie of the enemy that tells you, "This life is all there is. You might as well go out and enjoy it and satisfy your every need and desire, because when you die, that's it."

This life is not FOREVER. It is just a vapor — seen, then gone (James 4:14). It is like the grass that grows up and withers. Walk in the light of eternity. You are not going to be here forever.

When you feel like giving up, keep eternity in front of you and realize you have come too far to turn back now.

"Lay not up for yourselves treasures upon earth, where moth and rust doth corrupt, and where thieves break through and steal: But lay up for yourselves treasures in heaven, where neither moth nor rust doth corrupt, and where thieves do not break through nor steal" *(Matthew 6:19,20)*.

When the devil comes in with temptation offering passing pleasure, say, "No, devil, I prefer eternity around the throne of God. My God has prepared a mansion for me."

"In my Father's house are many mansions: if it were not so, I would have told you. I go to prepare a place for you. And if I go and prepare a place for you, I will come again, and receive you unto myself; that where I am, there ye may be also" *(John 14:2,3)*.

When the enemy tries to put his evil thoughts in your mind, say, "I do not think so, devil; I just do not think so."

Once you've caught sight of heaven — a glimpse of eternity kept ever before you — you can survive the onslaught of hell in this last day.

"For if we believe that Jesus died and rose again, even so them also which sleep in Jesus will God bring with him. For this we say unto

you by the word of the Lord, that we which are alive and remain unto the coming of the Lord shall not prevent them which are asleep. For the Lord himself shall descend from heaven with a shout, with the voice of the archangel, and with the trump of God: and the dead in Christ shall rise first: Then we which are alive and remain shall be caught up together with them in the clouds, to meet the Lord in the air: and so shall we ever be with the Lord" (1 Thessalonians 4:14-17).

"This old ship called "Zion" has withstood the deadening blows of the God-haters from the foundation of time, and it will continue to do so. "
-Pastor Rod Parsley

Jesus said, *"But as the days of Noe were, so shall also the coming of the Son of man be"* (Matthew 24:37).

I can see it now.

God told Noah, "Build me an ark."

He gave Noah the exact blueprint for deliverance.

God was giving a warning, "It is going to rain."

It had never rained before.

"Tell the people it is going to rain," God said. "Because of the corruption of the people, I am going to destroy them with a flood" (Genesis 6).

In the days of Noah, they were eating and drinking; they were violating their marriages; they were participating in revelry, in lawlessness, in lasciviousness. They were a people out of control and with no restraint.

The creation was separated from the Creator by sin, by agnosticism and by atheism.

But this old ship called "Zion" has withstood the deadening blows of the God-haters from the foundation of time, and it will continue to do so.

As it was in the days of Noah, so it will be today.

"And God said unto Noe, the end of all flesh is come before me; for the earth is filled with violence through them" (v. 13).

There was a message going out, but it was going unheeded by the people who needed it most.

It was not only a message of warning, but also of deliverance. Only Noah and his house would be saved, because only they had responded to God's instruction.

When the rains began to fall and the ark shifted and creaked off its wooden housing that had held it in place during construction, Noah and his family were safe inside. As the flood waters continued to rise, people clawed their fingers on the outside of that ark, screaming for deliverance. With water up around their necks, barely able to keep their mouths above water, they cried out, "We're drowning; we're dying!"

How strange it would have been in that hour for Noah to have lifted his hands, gathered his family around him like a chorus, and begun to sing "The Joy of the Lord", or maybe, "This is the Day" or maybe, "Something Good is Going to Happen to You."

How strange it is for men to climb on top of the ark of the anointing of God in the midst of a generation dying in the cesspool of its own self-indulgent sin, and begin to tell them, "Something good is going to happen."

Something good is not going to happen unless we discern the times, realize the day in which we're living, and cry out for a merciful God to be merciful to our sin-sick souls.

You <u>must</u> decide which side you're going to play on. You can't be the kickoff man on the devil's team and the receiving running back on God's team.

Make no mistake about it. There will come a time of ETERNAL accountability! Humble yourself and diligently seek God. Keep your eyes on eternity!

"Behold, the day of the Lord cometh, cruel both with wrath and fierce anger, to lay the land desolate: and he shall destroy the sinners thereof out of it. For the stars of heaven and the constellations thereof shall not give their light: the sun shall be darkened in his going forth, and the moon shall not cause her light to shine. And I will punish the world for their evil, and the wicked for their iniquity; and I will cause the arrogancy of the proud to cease, and will lay low the haughtiness of the terrible" (Isaiah 13:9-11).

*"For thus saith the high and lofty One that inhabiteth **eternity**, whose name is Holy; I dwell in the high and holy place, with him also that is of a contrite and humble spirit, to revive the spirit of the humble, and to revive the heart of the contrite ones" (Isaiah 57:15).*

Ask the Holy Spirit to help you stay humble and contrite before God, whose name is Holy! With your eyes focused on Him, you will soon (after the vapor of this life is over) dwell with Him in that "high and holy place."

STRATEGY FOUR

Be Vigilant

"Eternal vigilance is the price of freedom."
- Thomas Payne

"Be sober, be vigilant; because your adversary the devil, as a roaring lion, walketh about, seeking whom he may devour" (1 Peter 5:8).

"We must be vigilant and watchful. We must wake up spiritually and stay alert!"

- Pastor Rod Parsley

We must be vigilant to survive!

Too many of us want to run down to an altar and have some preacher tap us on the head with a little bit of oil, expecting every satanic assault will be stopped for the rest of our lives.

It is not going to happen that way.

Wake up and be vigilant over your own life, your own home.

Be watchful for the enemy; sound the spiritual alarm. Be able to identify him. You cannot be vigilant if you cannot recognize your enemy. Learn to recognize danger signs.

"For if the trumpet give an uncertain sound, who shall prepare himself to the battle?" (1 *Corinthians 14:8).*

Sodom and Gomorrha perished because they were not vigilant. They did not recognize the enemy of corruption that lied and deceived them into partaking in sinful pleasures.

"Even as Sodom and Gomorrha, and the cities about them in like manner, giving themselves over to fornication, and going after strange flesh, are set forth for an example, suffering the vengeance of eternal fire" (Jude 7).

The devil is plotting and planning your demise. Right now, he is scheming in his blighted mind what he can do to get you into a position of vulnerability — out from under the prayer cover of the protection of God. He's planning right now. He has a strategy. He's a spirit being; he doesn't need to sleep.

Speak the Word of God over your family and declare, "Devil, you're not having my teenager." When your children get ready for school, raise up a prayer cover over them that day so no crack dealer can give your thirteen year-old crack.

Be watchful, or sudden destruction will hit you when you least expect it.

"For when they shall say, Peace and safety; then sudden destruction cometh upon them, as travail upon a woman with child; and they shall not escape" (1 Thessalonians 5:3).

When is the last time you rebuked the spirit of divorce from your home? So many Christians expect everyone else to assume responsibility for their lives.

Wake up!

Gather your family together and sanctify your home unto God. Determine that nothing unholy, untrue, or unpure will enter the threshold of your home.

We must wake up spiritually and stay alert! Do not let the devil run rampant through your life!

"Wherefore let him that thinketh he standeth take heed lest he fall" (1 Corinthians 10:12).

Wake up and stay vigilant.

"We draw our strength from the battle. From our greatest conflicts come our greatest victories!

- Pastor Rod Parsley

It is time to roll up our sleeves, ready our bayonets, and realize we have an adversary who came to steal, kill, and destroy.

"The thief cometh not, but for to steal, and to kill, and to destroy: I am come that they might have life, and that they might have it more abundantly" (John 10:10).

The devil desires to stop us any way he can. Be receptive and responsive to the Word of God concerning the strategies of our adversary.

Understand how he works, and be vigilant to know his ways.

"To every thing there is a season, and a time to every purpose under the heaven. A time to be born, and a time to die; a time to plant, and a time to pluck up that which is planted" (Ecclesiastes 3:1,2).

Right before the end of this great passage, Solomon declared there is *"a time to love, and a time of hate; a time of war, and a time of peace" (Ecclesiastes 3:8).*

Be vigilant, for the devil has declared war. He does not rest. He wants to destroy you and your family.

Jesus, on the other hand, came to give you rest. He said, *"Peace I leave with you, my peace I give unto you: not as the world giveth, give I unto you. Let not your heart be troubled, neither let it be afraid" (John 14:27).*

Many Christians are running around today looking for peace. They do not want anything to disturb them. They want everything comfortable — but they do not want to maintain vigilance.

Christians want to think it's all right to just go to church, come back on Sunday night, sing and dance, go home and go to bed — and never raise up a prayer cover.

I pray along these lines every night before I go to bed:

"Father, into your hands I commend my mind. No force from without may attack my mind while I sleep. My mind will think only thoughts of blessing. Father, if there's anything that comes to my mind, it must be filtered through the sifting filter of the Holy Ghost and the Word of God. Right now, I raise up a prayer cover over my mind."

I lay hands on my children and pray over them every night:

"These children will sleep in the safety and peace of the covering of prayer that surrounds them. No supernatural force from the supernatural sphere, no principality, no power, no strategy, no design, no desire of the enemy can penetrate the cover of prayer I raise over them now, in Jesus' name."

We Christians are designed to be vigilant, to fight the good fight of faith, and enforce the Word of God in our own lives.

"Fight the good fight of faith, lay hold on eternal life, whereunto thou art also called, and hast professed a good profession before many witnesses" (1 Timothy 6:12).

We draw our strength from the battle. From our greatest conflicts come our greatest victories!

"Living on the inside of you is the Lion of the tribe of Judah. When He roars, let the devil be silenced."
— *Pastor Rod Parsley*

What does the Bible say Satan is doing?

"Be sober, be vigilant; because your adversary the devil, as a roaring lion, walketh about, seeking whom he may devour" (1 Peter 5:8).

Your adversary the devil, like a roaring lion, is seeking whom he may devour.

I have been studying about lions, and I discovered a lion will only roar under two circumstances.

One, he has not lost his teeth. A lion who has lost his teeth will never roar again!

The devil hasn't lost his teeth! He can still bite, kill, steal, and destroy. He will wreak havoc in your life if you do not get serious about surviving. It is time for us to stop playing church. It is time for us to stand up and recognize we have an adversary, and we must be on CONSTANT WATCH to discern his wicked ways!

Two, a lion only roars when he is hungry. Scripture says the devil is hungry. He is out there — roaming to and fro seeking whom he may devour.

The devil is out to get you, and he is relentless in his pursuit. He is crafty and cunning, and he is the master of deception.

"Take heed that ye be not deceived" (Luke 21:8).

Wake up!

We have an adversary, and he will kill you any way he can if you let him.

When a lion roars, every other animal in the entire animal kingdom stops in its tracks and comes to complete silence. The only other creature that would dare make a sound after a lion has roared is another lion.

The Lion of the tribe of Judah lives on the inside of every born again believer. When He roars, let the devil be silenced!"

And one of the elders saith unto me, weep not: behold, the Lion of the tribe of Judah, the Root of David, hath prevailed to open the book, and to loose the seven seals thereof" (Revelation 5:5).

"It is time we circled the wagons, pulled out the artillery, rolled up our sleeves, and readied ourselves to be tough with the devil."

- Pastor Rod Parsley

The devil is not a little man in a red suit with a pitchfork and horns.

He is Satan — the thief, the master deceiver, the murderer!

He is behind every heinous crime ever committed, and he will damn your soul to hell if you let him. He will rape your family, steal your finances, and leave you on the trash heap of wreck and ruin ... if you let him.

Jesus said to His friends, *"But I will forewarn you whom ye shall fear: Fear him, which after he hath killed hath power to cast into hell: yea, I say unto you, Fear him" (Luke 12:5).*

The devil hates you.

He wants preachers fighting with preachers; he wants Christians fighting with Christians.

He will do anything he can to destroy us.

He will sit a person delivered from alcoholism on an airplane and have a stewardess offer him a drink fifteen times.

He will get you if he can.

This is your wake-up alarm!

We are in a spiritual battlefield, not a heavenly recreation room. We are facing the very forces of hell.

Understand right now that the devil is out to stop you. Get this settled in your spirit. It is time to get serious if we are going to survive.

It is time we circled the wagons, pulled out the artillery, rolled up our sleeves, and readied ourselves to be tough with the devil.

STRATEGY FIVE

Stay "Tuned" to the Spirit

"For as many as are led by the Spirit of God, they are the sons of God" (Romans 8:14).

"There's more to me than what you can see with your eyes. In the spirit, I look like a giant."

- Pastor Rod Parsley

When you are born again, you are born of the Spirit (John 3). There's something inside you greater than what is wrapped around you.

We are spirit beings. We have been born of the eternal Word of God, and that seed remains in us. We are eternal, invincible, indestructible.

You say, "Not so. I could take out a gun and shoot you in the head, and you'd die." Yes, but I would still be alive. To to be absent from the body is to be present with the Lord (2 Corinthians 5:8).

We do have a struggle; it is the battle of the ages — but you can survive this battle.

Get in touch with that part of you that's born of God.

Get in tune with your spirit.

The Bible says the spirit of a man shall sustain all his infirmity — including the weakness of his flesh (Proverb 18:14). That's the reason I do not believe born again people who say "the devil made me do it. I was weak. I fell into sin."

That is impossible. You cannot fall into sin. The Bible plainly says he makes your feet like hind's feet and keeps you from falling (Psalm 18:33).

It's time to get some serious survival strategies. Understand that we are spirit beings!

There's more to me than what you can see with your eyes. In the spirit, I look a giant.

The spirit man in most Christians is emaciated. In the spirit realm, they are like starving refugees, little tiny beings with knees bigger than their thighs.

Your natural man wakes up and says, "It's breakfast time," and at noon, "It's lunch time," and in the evening, "It's supper time," and every hour in between, "It's snack time."

But many don't even look at their Bibles outside church service. Just like the natural man eats natural food to live, the spirit man must receive spirit food to live.

To stay in tune in the spirit, you have to feed your spirit.

Your spirit lives by faith.

Faith is not a spare tire tool to get us out of tragic situations.

Galatians 3:11 tells us, *"The just shall live by faith."*

Hebrews 11:1 tells us that faith is the substance of things hoped for, the evidence of things that cannot be seen or perceived with the natural senses.

Get in tune with your spirit if you plan to survive!

If you're going to survive the perils of perilous times, you need to have a faith that knows. You need to have a faith that grows. You need to have a faith that's rooted.

Faith is the conduit from heaven to earth. It is the sixth sense God gives you. The hand of faith reaches into the realm of the spirit and pulls whatever you need into the natural.

A natural man is born by the joining together of the seed of the man and egg of the woman. That egg is alive, but it's abiding in a state of death. If it is not touched by the seed of the man, it will be cast off.

When the seed of the man touches the egg of the woman, conception takes place. Conception is the joining of that which is without to that which is within, producing a new offspring.

We have the same hope the egg of that woman has. The only way for it to live is to receive something in itself from without. Something outside has to get in ... and that something is the incorruptible seed of the Word of God.

That Word can't get planted in your mind; it will die there.

It's like the seed sown on stony ground. The sun comes up and bakes it dry because it has no root. When the first trial — the first problem — comes your way, you give up on God because all you have is mental assent.

You must be born of the Spirit (see John 3). That's the reason the Bible says, "the things of the spirit are ... enmity to the carnal mind.

"For to be carnally minded is death; but to be spiritually minded is life and peace. Because the carnal mind is enmity against God; for it is not subject to the law of God, neither indeed can be" (Romans 8:6,7).

They that are in the flesh cannot please God. It's absolutely impossible.

Feed your spirit with the Word of God. Keep your spirit strong with the Word of God to survive the attacks of the devil.

Unless you learn to be led by your spirit, you will follow the dictates your mind, and you will follow the dictates of your flesh.

Get in tune with your spirit. Walk in the Spirit of God, clothed with the mind of God.

"So then they that are in the flesh cannot please God. But ye are not in the flesh, but in the Spirit, if so be that the Spirit of God dwell in you. Now if any man have not the Spirit of Christ, he is none of his. And if Christ be in you, the body is dead because of sin" (Romans 8:8-10).

If you are led by the Spirit, if you're in tune to the Spirit, your body is reckoned dead. You cannot tempt a dead body.

The Spirit of God dwells in us, making the appetites of the flesh and soul dead, as we give Him expression in our lives. As we allow the Spirit to dwell in us moment by moment, day by day, week after week, year after year, it is continually separating us and setting us apart.

Too often we are not tuned in. We do not give the Spirit an opportunity to express His nature.

"Therefore, brethren, we are debtors, not to flesh to live after the flesh" (Romans 8:12).

God is saying, "Hey, you don't owe your flesh anything! When it cries out, "You owe me a piece of coconut cream pie," when it cries out, "I want to be sick" — remember, you can overcome temptation if you are in tune with your spirit.

"Greater is he that is in you than he that is in the world" (1 John 4:4).

Start overcoming temptation, and the devil will tuck his tail and run. Feed your spirit with the Word of God. Get in touch with that life on the inside of you. Feel it! Feel it bubbling up! Feel its joy! Feel its power! Feel its authority! Feel its ability! It's bigger than you! It's greater than you!

"You can base your life on who God is, what God is, and what God says."

- Pastor Rod Parsley

God is accurate in His communication with us. By staying in tune with the Holy Spirit, and we learn to be "accurate". His Spirit keeps us "on target" to those things He wants for our life.

Malachi is the last book of the Old Covenant, and I have always found last words very interesting. Malachi is God's last statement before 400 years of silence. If you were not going to talk again for 400 years, the last thing you had to say would be very significant.

God said, *"And I will come near to you to judgment; and I will be a swift witness against ... those that ... fear not me, saith the Lord of Hosts. For I am the Lord, I change not; therefore ye sons of Jacob are not consumed"* (Malachi 3:5,6).

God said His laws and covenants never change. Your spiritual target is always the same, and you will never miss it if your spirit is strong.

God said that who He is, and what He is, and what He has said ... never changes.

Many Christians want to change God; they want Him to conform to their own idolatrous image of who they think He is. They want to form a molten calf, a graven image on the inside of their own hearts, of a God that fits into their own particular lifestyle.

God steps right in the middle of that scenario and says, "Hold on. Wait just a minute. It does not matter what you think about your situation; I will never change. It does not matter how you try to mold me; I will never change. It does not matter what men say about me, or what philosophy says, or what religion says ... I will never change."

"Jesus Christ the same yesterday, and to day, and for ever. Be not carried about with divers and strange doctrines. For it is a good thing that the heart be established with grace; not with meats, which have not profited them that have been occupied therein" (Hebrews 13:8,9).

You can base your life on who God is, what God is, and what God says. The only stability in this whole universe is: God will never change.

Keep your eye on the mark, and you will hit the spiritual target every single time!

"I press toward the mark for the prize of the high calling of God in Christ Jesus. Let us therefore, as many as be perfect, be thus minded: and if in any thing ye be otherwise minded, God shall reveal even this unto you" (Philippians 3:14,15).

Paul was saying, "I have my spiritual target clearly in my spirit, and it is to be like Jesus

Christ. And if my mind ever starts to veer from that target, I rely on the Holy Spirit to reveal to me the error of my way."

If our lives are to be steadfast, we must walk in tune with the Holy Spirit that reflects God's truth.

"I never want to hear said I have to die and cannot live; therefore, I get up in the morning and I am watchful."

- Pastor Rod Parsley

Being in tune with the Spirit will save your life.

Wake up!

You have an adversary.

Stay in tune with your Heavenly Father through the Holy Spirit, and you will know when that adversary attempts to attack you and your family.

You say, "I do not know how this cancer got in my body."

Wake up!

The devil had a plan, and you did not do anything to counteract it. Often, I wake up in the morning and say, "Thank you, God, for healing me of cancer."

"You have never had cancer," you say.

That is exactly my point — I have never had it, and I do not ever intend to have it! I never want to hear said I have to die and cannot live; therefore, I get up in the morning and I am watchful. I ask the Holy Spirit to keep me in tune with His holy will for my life.

I say, "Devil, no cancer cell can live in my body. If while I was asleep one invaded my body, it has to leave now, in the name of Jesus. My bloodstream is cleansed; my mind is alert; my bones and tissues function properly; my heart is strong; my lungs are strong."

What am I doing?

I am watching and staying on target with the spiritual realities in my life.

I am deflecting fiery darts with the powerful shield of faith.

"Above all, taking the shield of faith, wherewith ye shall be able to quench all the fiery darts of the wicked" (Ephesians 6:16).

If I am watchful, walking in tune with the Holy Spirit, I will survive hell's onslaught in these last days.

"You get involved in hope beyond the scope of natural human limitation when you begin to pray in the Holy Ghost."

- Pastor Rod Parsley

You are a man born of the Spirit.

"As many as are led by the Spirit of God, they are the sons of God" (Romans 8:14).

When you are led by the Spirit, you can traverse the storms of life — the perils of perilous times — and come out on the other side.

Your clothes will not smell like smoke even though you go through the fire. The Holy Ghost of God knows how to get us through the treacherous fires and furnaces set ablaze by the enemy.

He knows where the icebergs are — just underneath the surface — perils you cannot see with your natural eyes.

As we operate in the spiritual realm, "looking to Jesus" as our guide, we have authority to command demon power to release every hold on us, on our families, and our lives.

Use your spiritual ammunition.

"I will pray with the spirit, and I will pray with the understanding also: I will sing with the spirit, and I will sing with the understanding also" (1 Corinthians 14:15).

Learn to pray in the Holy Ghost for the perfect will of the Father to be accomplished in your life.

"Do not blame your inconsistencies on God; He has never failed. He has never lost a battle. You are in a Kingdom that <u>cannot be shaken</u>."
-Pastor Rod Parsley

God has given us His gifts to help keep us accurate in our spiritual walk — to help us flow in His will.

"But the manifestation of the Spirit is given to every man to profit withal. For to one is given by the Spirit the word of wisdom; to another the word of knowledge by the same Spirit; To another faith by the same Spirit; to another the gifts of healing by the same Spirit; To another the working of miracles; to another prophecy; to another discerning of spirits; to another divers kinds of tongues; to another the interpretation of tongues:" (1 Corinthians 12:7-10).

If you do not understand the gifts of the Spirit, how are they going to operate in your life?

If they are not operational, when some little trial hits you, will you fall apart? Will you run out of the Kingdom of God saying these gifts do not work?

If you do not know how to do algebra, you do not run around saying "Algebra does not work." Instead, you would say, "I do not know how to do algebra."

Do not blame your inconsistencies on God; He has never failed. He has never lost a battle. He is so accurate that He NEVER misses the mark!

You are in a Kingdom that cannot be shaken. *"In the multitude of my thoughts within me thy comforts delight my soul" (Psalm 94:19).*

Did you ever have a time when it just seemed like everything was going wrong, and your anxious thoughts were multiplied within you? You tossed on the bed of trial and tribulation, and you could not sleep. You did not know what to do, and you could not pray anymore.

Then be honest with God.

He said anxious thoughts, troubling thoughts are multiplied.

The Psalmist said that when you are going through the perils of perilous times and your soul is out of control, seek the comforts of God!

There is hope for you beyond the borders of human limitation. God and His Word are not bound. You may be bound, but the Word of God is not bound, and it shall give you life.

"It is the spirit that quickeneth; the flesh profiteth nothing: the words that I speak unto you, they are spirit, and they are life" (John 6:63).

Jesus gave His life for you so that you might walk in salvation and life.

"No one takes it [my life] away from Me. On the contrary, I lay it down voluntarily. I ... have power to lay it down and I am authorized and have power to take it back again" (John 10:18 AMP).

In the natural, Jesus was swung up on a cross, hung between heaven and hell, looking like a sacrificial animal. When they took Him from the cross, they brushed His blood-soaked, matted hair. They wrapped Him in grave clothes, put Him in the borrowed tomb of Joseph of Arimathaea, and rolled a stone in front of the burial place.

The hopes and dreams of the disciples were shattered.

But Jesus said to that grave, *"Lift up your heads, O ye gates; and be ye lift up, ye everlasting doors; and the King of glory shall come in" (Psalm 24:7).*

Jesus stood looking at death, but He knew the hope of glory.

"Knowing that Christ being raised from the dead dieth no more; death hath no more dominion over him" (Romans 6:9).

Jesus had the power to survive the perils of perilous times and lift up His eyes beyond the seen into the unseen. He stared death in the face and said, "The Word of the Lord is in Me, and death cannot hold me."

The Living Word of God is inside you today in the form of the Holy Spirit.

You can survive these perilous times because He is there to guide you, to keep you on target, to keep you pressing forward toward the mark in all things.

No circumstances can hold you or keep you down as you press forward toward the high calling.

"I press toward the mark for the prize of the high calling of God in Christ Jesus" (Philippians 3:14).

Jesus — the Living Word — broke through apparent defeat into glorious victory.

Stay tuned to the Holy Spirit, and trust Him to bring you safely through!

Realize Spiritual Warfare is _the_ War

Only 268 Years of Peace in 4,000 Years

"Someone has taken the time to review the history of war and learned that in the last 4,000 years, there have been but 268 years entirely free from war. This, of course, only takes into consideration 'man's inhumanity to man'; for if man's inhumanity to God were to be considered, it would have to be said there has not been a single moment from the fall of man to the present minute that has been entirely free from war."

- Gospel Herald

"Ye shall not need to fight in this battle: set yourselves, stand ye still, and see the salvation of the Lord with you, O Judah and Jerusalem: fear not, nor be dismayed; to morrow go out against them: for the Lord will be with you" _(2 Chronicles 20:17)._

"Do not write letters to our men of God saying, 'I am deeply sorry you fell.' Instead, write them letters that say, 'I am sorry I let go.'"

- Pastor Rod Parsley

All twelve disciples had the joy of walking and talking with Jesus while He lived on the face of this earth. He loved them, and they all loved Him.

Matthew was a tax collector, but he gave up his profession to follow Jesus.

John was a fisherman, but he gave up his fishing business to follow Jesus.

Yet, Jesus said specifically to Peter, "Satan wants you" (Luke 22:31,32).

Jesus was serious about His mission, and He understood the nature of the enemy. The devil did not have his eyes focused on Matthew or John. Jesus said, "Simon, Satan has desired to have you," because Jesus understood that Satan wanted to attack the very foundation — the rock — of the church.

Peter was a church leader, so he was a prime target for the forces of hell!

I recently heard someone say, "Well, it disturbs me that there have been so many so-called church leaders who have fallen into sin."

Friend, this is spiritual warfare.

Let us put the responsibility where it belongs: these leaders have not fallen as much as we dropped them!

The Bible says, *"Confess your faults one to another, and pray one for another, that ye may be healed. The effectual fervent prayer of a righteous man availeth much" (James 5:16).*

If the body of Christ had been serious about the church and about its leaders, then we would have been praying earnestly for God to protect them, just as Jesus prayed earnestly for protection upon Peter.

Jesus knew the importance of prayer. In the Garden of Gethsemane, He revealed to His disciples this vital key to spiritual survival. Jesus was facing the greatest battle of His life as He looked toward the suffering, shame, and death of the cross. He went up to the Mount of Olives to pray. He knew He needed to be strengthened in prayer. He knew He needed spiritual energy to face what was before Him.

Before He entered into a time of prayer and travail before God, He told His disciples, *"Pray that ye enter not into temptation" (Luke 22:40).*

You know the rest of the story. The apostles fell asleep.

Today, I believe we often are spiritually asleep, not realizing that Satan is lurking just around the corner, ready to attack us and our spiritual leaders at any moment. It is up to us to undergird them in prayer.

It may be that our spiritual leaders have not fallen. Perhaps we have dropped them from our prayer petitions to God Almighty!

Instead of writing letters to our men of God saying, "I am deeply sorry you fell," we may need to write them letters that say, "I am sorry I let go."

Do not become caught up on the bandwagon of preacher-bashing and believer-bashing. Never turn your spiritual machine gun on the very people fighting with you in the same Army of God. It is time to quit killing our wounded, and extend our hand of support to our wounded foxhole buddies.

We need the foot soldiers and we need the generals if we are to defeat the enemy in every battle.

"Well, Pastor Rod," you reply, "that is easy for you to say. But the simple fact is there are many who have fallen from grace who did not do everything just right."

Do you?

"He that is without sin among you, let him first cast a stone at her" (John 8:7).

When no one was willing to stone the woman who was in adultery, Jesus asked the woman, *"Woman, where are those thine accusers? hath no man condemned thee?" (John 8:10).*

The woman replied, *"No man, Lord. And Jesus said unto her, Neither do I condemn thee: go, and sin no more" (John 8:11).*

I see the broken lives of believers all around me, but I do not — and cannot — place the blame on them. Instead, the Holy Spirit leads me to pray, "God, help me hold on tighter. Let me take hold of the horns of the altar; let me thwart every satanic opposition against their lives, in the name of Jesus."

A great general once said "War is hell."

In the realm of the spirit, his words are only too true. Our war is literally against hell and all it stands for; and we must not ever forget it.

Pray for those who have fallen. Ask God to be merciful in His judgment, and to restore them back into His grace. Remember, God's judgment is far fairer than any we can impose, and it is a judgment to be feared by those who refuse to walk in His precepts.

"He that despised Moses' law died without mercy under two or three witnesses: Of how much sorer punishment, suppose ye, shall he be thought worthy, who hath trodden under foot the son of God, and hath counted the blood of the covenant, wherewith he was sanctified, an unholy thing, and hath done despite unto the Spirit of grace? For we know him that hath said,

Vengeance belongeth unto me, I will recompense, saith the Lord. And again, The Lord shall judge his people. It is a fearful thing to fall into the hands of the living God" (Hebrews 10:28-31).

Learn Your Weapons

Excellence

"The quality of a person's life is in direct proportion to their commitment to excellence, regardless of their chosen field of endeavor."

- Author Unknown

Persistence

"Nothing in the world can take the place of persistence. Talent will not; nothing is more common than unsuccessful men with talent. Genius will not; unrewarded genius is almost a proverb. Education will not; the world is full of educated derelicts. Persistence and determination are omnipotent."

- Author Unknown

"Wherefore take unto you the whole armour of God, that ye may be able to withstand in the evil day, and having done all, to stand. Stand therefore, having your loins girt about with truth, and having on the breastplate of righteousness; And your feet shod with the preparation of the gospel of peace; Above all, taking the shield of

faith, wherewith ye shall be able to quench all the fiery darts of the wicked. And take the helmet of salvation, and the sword of the Spirit, which is the word of God" (Ephesians 6:13-17).

"Samson had anointed power for spiritual battle as long as he lived within his covenant. Even when no other weapon was available, he was able to use the jawbone of an ass to slay his enemies."
- Pastor Rod Parsley

The first rule in developing skill with the weapons of the spirit is to use what is familiar. It is not how extensive your spiritual tool box is, but rather, your ability to build a spiritual house with the tools available to you.

David, when trying on Saul's armor, said, "Thanks, but no thanks. I am sure it is good armor, but is not comfortable for me. By the way, Saul, this armor has not done much for you lately, either."

"And David said unto Saul, I cannot go with these [your armor]; for I have not proved them. And David put them off him" (1 Samuel 17:39).

Instead of using Saul's armor, David chose his own weapons — weapons that were tried in the heat of battle. David took with him familiar weapons. He had "proven" his sling. He had killed a lion and a bear as evidence that he was familiar with his weapon.

David understood what his sling could do, and he fully understood the power of the God he served.

"Then said David to the Philistine, Thou comest to me with a sword, and with a spear, and with a shield: but I come to thee in the name of the Lord of hosts, the God of the armies of Israel, whom thou hast defiled" (1 Samuel 17:45).

David knew he had the right weapon, and he was ready to use it.

David knew he had the right God — the very Lord of Hosts, and he was ready to serve Him!

The second rule in learning how to properly use your spiritual weapons is to develop your spiritual strength. No matter how skillful a soldier is with his weapon, an exhausted 98 pound weakling cannot defeat his foe over the long course of battle.

You need constant and continual spiritual exercise to build and maintain your strength!

"But strong meat belongeth to them that are of full age, even those who by reason of use have their senses exercised to discern both good and evil" (Hebrews 5:14).

Do you see it? The strong become that way by exercise, by "reason of use." God has given you spiritual senses to discern the enemy and discern your fellow warriors ... exercise those senses.

If you have the power of God's anointing on your life, you can defeat the devil by learning how to use the spiritual weapons He has given you, and by exercising your spirit man to stay fit for battle.

Samson had anointed power for battle as long as he lived within his covenant. Even when no other weapon was available, he was able to use the jawbone of an ass to slay his enemies.

"And he found a new jawbone of an ass, and put forth his hand, and took it, and slew a thousand men therewith" (Judges 15:15).

The third rule in using spiritual weapons is to live within your covenant. Samson had power as long as he lived within his covenant.

It is essential to understand that no matter how skillful we become with our weapons, weapon familiarity is not the true source of our strength. Our power (anointing) rests in personal holiness and our relationship to God ... how closely we stay within His covenant.

"For this is the covenant that I will make with the house of Israel after those days, saith the Lord; I will put my laws into their mind, and write them in their hearts: and I will be to them a God, and they shall be to me a people" (Hebrews 8:10).

Saul, though ever so skillful with a sword and spear, was out of covenant with his God, and so Goliath humiliated him.

Goliath had a valiant war record, but as an uncircumcised Philistine, he was not in covenant with God. David understood his covenant relationship, and triumphed.

"Let us draw near with a true heart in full assurance of faith, having our hearts sprinkled from an evil conscience, and our bodies washed with pure water. Let us hold fast the profession of our faith without wavering; (for he is faithful that promised;) And let us consider one another to provoke unto love and to good works" (Hebrews 10:22-24).

Purity and a true heart are the spiritual keys to unlocking the power of God in your life. Have faith that He will stand by your side in any battle, and always operate within the guidelines of His loving covenant.

God is absolutely pure, therefore, He is absolutely powerful.

Oil has power, but refined in purity to diesel fuel, its power is greatly increased and intensified. As that oil is further processed and purified into gasoline, its power is increased many fold.

"...neither be partaker of other men's sins: keep thyself pure" (1 Timothy 5:22).

Remember, in spiritual warfare, purity means power.

"The Bible doesn't say 'if the enemy comes in'; it says 'when the enemy comes in.' I am getting ready for the onslaughts of hell."
- Pastor Rod Parsley

Some time back, we had an evangelistic power team at our church. Early in the day, they were walking around with bowls of food in their hands.

I said, "What do you have in the bowls?"

They showed me — boiled spaghetti with nothing on it, boiled potatoes with nothing on them. And they had big chunks of bread.

They would grab a potato, then they would grab some spaghetti, then they would start in on the bread.

They ate it all.

That's part of the price they paid to be weight lifters.

Watching them, I suddenly realized "That is what I must look like in the spirit!"

I grab some of the Word for my food.

"But he was wounded for our transgressions, he was bruised for our iniquities: the chastisement of our peace was upon him; and with his stripes we are healed" (Isaiah 53:5).

I get a quick bite of spiritual energy.

"But my God shall supply all your need according to his riches in glory by Christ Jesus" (Philippians 4:19).

When I am going from my house to my office, I carry along a bowl of living water to quench my thirsty spirit.

"For it is written, He shall give his angels charge over thee, to keep thee: And in their hands they shall bear thee up, lest at any time thou dash thy foot against a stone" (Luke 4:10).

What am I doing?

Day and night, no matter what I am doing, I continually feed my spirit man.

Do I need the nourishment right this second?

No, but I am storing it up.

The Bible doesn't say "if the enemy comes in"; it says "when the enemy comes in."

I am getting ready for the onslaughts of hell. When they come, I will have the muscle power to defeat every adversary because I was faithful to feed my spirit man.

You are a spirit.

And that spirit man needs to be fed!

We know our bodies need to be fed, and we carefully plan our meals while we go through the shopping line.

"Oh, I will buy some of these spices, because next Thursday I am going to have hot chicken wings. And on Friday, I am going to have roast beef. And then, I better not buy anything for Saturday night, because that is when we go out for pizza. On next Monday, I think I will have some fried tomatoes and some salad greens."

The same methodical approach needs to apply to how you feed your spirit.

When you walk through a Christian bookstore, say to yourself, "Well, on Monday, I think I will have some gifts of the Holy Ghost. On Tuesday, I will try some of that prayer without ceasing. On Friday, that is warfare day; I think I will have some hallelujah warfare preaching. Let me see, what else am I going to need this week? Oh, I think I need some of those healing tapes. This is flu season."

There is a spiritual assault coming from the corridors of hell, and you need to learn how to feed your spirit man. You need to fortify yourself with strong spiritual ammunition.

Get ready! Feed your spirit man by abiding in the shadow of the Almighty.

"He that dwelleth in the secret place of the most High shall abide under the shadow of the Almighty. I will say of the Lord, He is my refuge and my fortress: my God; in him will I trust. Surely he shall deliver thee from the snare of the fowler, and from the noisome pestilence" (Psalm 91:1-3).

"Study to shew thyself approved unto God, a workman that needeth not to be ashamed, rightly dividing the word of truth" *(2 Timothy 2:15).*

To feed your spirit man, study the Word of God. Memorize it. Let it sink deep into your spirit. It is the most tangible and powerful weapon God has given us for our spiritual arsenal.

"For the word of God is quick, and powerful, and sharper than any two-edged sword, piercing even to the dividing asunder of soul and spirit, and of the joints and marrow, and is a discerner of the thoughts and intents of the heart" *(Hebrews 4:12).*

"I believe we are heading toward the imminent return of the King of Kings and the Lord of Lords. I believe Jesus is coming."
                                    - Pastor Rod Parsley

The spiritual warfare of these last days involves all the weapons and all the armaments of the spirit. We are living in the last hours of the last days.

"But of that day and hour knoweth no man, no, not the angels of heaven, but my Father only" (Matthew 24:36).

Jesus said that even though we would not know the day and hour of His return, we would know the season. I pray you understand the relevance and urgency of the message that God has deposited in my spirit for this endtime season.

It is time to get ready!

Something is about to happen.

I believe those chariots that have not ridden the wind since the days of Elijah are being polished by the heavenly hosts, being prepared to be pulled out of their stalls.

I believe we are heading toward the imminent return of the King of Kings and the Lord of Lords.

I believe Jesus is coming ... soon.

It is time for the church to become the glorious church of the book of Ephesians, instead of the lukewarm Laodicean church that the book of Revelation reveals.

"Unto the angel of the church of Ephesus write; These things saith he that holdeth the seven stars in his right hand, who walketh in the midst of the seven golden candlesticks; I know thy works, and thy labour, and thy patience, and how thou canst not bear them which are evil: and thou hast tried them which say they are apostles, and are not, and hast found them liars: And has borne, and hast patience, and for my name's sake hast laboured, and hast not fainted" (Revelation 2:1-3).

I pray that the church today will mirror the church of Ephesus, and recognize we are in a spiritual war. As we fight this war, I pray God will see that we are strong, and that even in the heaviest attacks of the enemies, we do not faint!

"Well, we are in the middle of revival," some Christians say, "and there is a great outpouring."

Yet, other Christians claim, "This is one of the coldest, darkest days ever in the history of the church. We are a dead church in the middle of a dying world."

Which is it?

A close examination of the Word of God will reveal that in the hour you and I are living in, the cold are going to get colder and the hot are going to get hotter.

"I know thy works, that thou art neither cold nor hot: I would thou wert cold or hot. So then because thou art lukewarm, and neither cold nor hot, I will spue thee out of my mouth" *(Revelation 3:15,16).*

There is going to be a verifiable polarization of the kingdom of darkness and the Kingdom of Light. You are going to walk in one kingdom or the other — so walk in the light.

"In him was life; and the life was the light of men. And the light shineth in darkness; and the darkness comprehended it not" (John 1:4,5).

Live in God's Radiance

My Father is Here

"I had a friend who was very happy in the possession of a beautiful wife, and a sweet little daughter of the age of three. Sudden sorrow struck the home when the young wife was killed in a traffic accident, and it seemed that all of the light had gone out of his life forever.

"The night after the funeral, the young father was putting his baby daughter to bed, and with awkward fingers was buttoning her sleeping garment when the lights suddenly went out all over the house. He suspected that a fuse had blown out in the basement, and said to the baby, 'Papa will be right back; you lie still and wait here.'

"But she, frightened at the thought of being left alone, pleaded to be taken with him, so he picked her up in his arms and started through the darkened hallway and down the stairs. The babe snuggled in his arms for a while in silence; but as they entered the basement she tightened her arms about his neck, and said, 'It is awfully dark; but I am not afraid, because my papa is here!'

"A sob shook the man's whole body. He buried his face in the baby's hair and wept, as he said, 'Yes, dear, it is dark, indeed; but I also am not afraid because my Father is here!'"

- Bible Expositor and Illuminator

Certainly I Will Be With Thee

"Many years ago, a little boy lay on his small bed, having just retired for the night. Before going to sleep, he moved in the direction of the large bed on which his father lay, and said, 'Father, are you there?' and the answer came back, 'Yes, my son.' I remember that that boy turned over and went to sleep without a thought of harm.

"Tonight that little boy is an old man of seventy, and every night before going to sleep he looks up into the face of his Heavenly Father and says, 'Father, are You there?' and the answer comes back clear and strong, 'Yes, My son.'

"Whom need we fear if God our Father is with us?"

- Scattered Seed

"As we draw close to God and spend time in His presence, we take on His radiance and character."

- Pastor Rod Parsley

"Submit yourselves therefore to God. Resist the devil, and he will flee from you. Draw nigh to God, and he will draw nigh to you. Cleanse your hands, ye sinners; and purify your hearts, ye double minded" (James 4:7,8).

Drawing close to God is the essential key to making the devil flee from you.

The key to successful resistance is to draw close to God!

"And the children of Israel saw the face of Moses, that the skin of Moses' face shone: and Moses put the veil upon his face again, until he went in to speak with him" (Exodus 34:35).

Moses spent time with God, and the very holiness of God permeated his face so that it actually radiated the glory of the Almighty!

Jesus was the express image, the living radiance, of the Father.

"Who being the brightness of his glory, and the express image of his person, and upholding all things by the word of his power, when he had by himself purged our sins, sat down on the right hand of the Majesty on high" (Hebrews 1:3).

The word "image" in this Scripture comes from the Greek word "charakter" and means "character." This was a term used in making coins. A metal disk, usually gold or silver, was heated in a hot flame. The desired mold or image was then placed over it and struck with a hammer. This striking process placed the image on the mold deep into the softened metal disk.

We see three things here.

One, to become His express image, to draw near to our Holy God, we must be heated by the fire. This is done in one of two ways: either in the heat of the glory of His presence or in the heat of adversity and persecution.

I believe Christians could avoid a lot of adversity if they would allow their lives to be softened in the heat of His glory.

But one way or the other, by glory or by adversity, we will have to be softened if we are to take on His image.

"Yea, and all that will live godly in Christ Jesus shall suffer persecution" (2 Timothy 3:12).

Two, to become His express image — no matter how soft or yielded we are — we must come into personal and intimate contact with Him to receive His image.

God wants us to be in a close relationship with Him.

"I am the good shepherd: the good shepherd giveth his life for the sheep. But he that is an hireling, and not the shepherd, whose own the sheep are not, seeth the wolf coming, and leaveth

the sheep, and fleeth: and the wolf catcheth them, and scattereth the sheep. The hireling fleeth, because he is an hireling, and careth not for the sheep. I am the good shepherd, and know my sheep, and am known of mine" (John 10:11-14).

If we do not have a personal relationship with God, when the wolf comes (the devil) we will flee from fear. But as we "know" God, we will have the strength to defeat Satan in our daily battles.

Three, there will be a striking process where the character of God is branded into our spirits.

It may come as a shock to you, but while resting in Jesus' arms, you might suddenly experience a sharp spiritual blow that will drive you so close to Jesus that His image is stamped permanently upon you.

That stamp allows you to receive His mind, His love, His wisdom, and His glory.

"But we all, with open face beholding as in a glass the glory of the Lord, are changed into the same image from glory to glory, even as by the Spirit of the Lord" (2 Corinthians 3:18).

To be holy and to survive in this decade of devastation and doom, we must be sealed in the sanctity of God through His Holy Spirit.

"And grieve not the holy Spirit of God, whereby we are sealed unto the day of redemption" (Ephesians 4:30).

"In the midst of the trials of life, it is one thing to know God as Deliverer, Helper, Comforter. It is another thing to have God say, 'I know this man.'"

- Pastor Rod Parsley

I shared with you earlier how the devil will especially attack men like Peter — men who are chosen by God to be His spiritual leaders.

And the devil will also attack you.

In these times of personal attack, it is essential that we each stay close to God, obey His precepts, and bask in His holiness and power.

Clint Brown, our music minister, was ready to leave his home on the day he would be involved in a car accident, and although he never wears a seat belt, he just felt something telling him to put it on that day. The impact of the accident would have sent him through his windshield and into the windshield of the other car. Clint is alive today and serving God; the police officer said he surely would have been dead at the scene if he had not been wearing his seat belt.

Was it just a little inward intuition that caused him to put his seat belt on?

Was it the time he spent the night before, consecrating his life and ministry to the Lord?

Or was it one of the members of our church climbing out of bed at four o'clock on the morning of the accident, kneeling by the bed and weeping tears of intercession in the Holy Ghost, praying for our staff?

I do not know for sure what happened, but I do know our music minister was preserved through the power of God!

When Jesus told Simon Peter, "Satan hath requisitioned and received permission to have you," it could not have been good news to Peter.

How would you like to receive that great prophetic message from God today?

"Satan asked if he could have you, and I said, 'Take him; take your best shot.'"

God trusted Simon Peter.

Today, as you mature in your faith, God trusts you because you are striving to be ONE in holiness with HIM.

God said something to the devil that I pray every person will one day hear from the lips of our Heavenly Father:

"And the Lord said unto Satan, Hast thou considered my servant Job, that there is none like him in the earth, a perfect and upright man, one that feareth God, and escheweth evil? and still he holdeth fast his integrity...."

The devil presented himself before God and said about Job, "Skin for skin, yea, all that a man hath will he give for his life. But put forth thine hand now, and touch his bone and his flesh, and he will curse thee to thy face" (Job 2:3-5).

God said, "Not so, I know the man; I know him."

In the midst of the trials of life, it is one thing to know God, to know Him as deliverer, helper, comforter. It is another thing to have God say, "I know this man, I know his heart, and I know he will faithfully serve me."

I want to be that man.

"When you are born again and filled with the Holy Ghost and start talking in tongues, the world might not want to rub shoulders with you anymore."

- Pastor Rod Parsley

Job trusted God and stayed holy and faithful in the midst of trial. When trials hit your life, God wants you to trust Him and maintain a deep relationship so that you can experience His power and blessing.

"Having therefore these promises, dearly beloved, let us cleanse ourselves from all filthiness of the flesh and spirit, perfecting holiness in the fear of God" (2 Corinthians 7:1).

What if the devil took away your house?

Your lands?

Your kids?

What about your gold-plated reputation?

What if the devil took that away from you and you could not ever get it back? After all, once a lie is told, it is told — it is impossible to untell it.

How do you unscramble eggs?

The more you try, the bigger mess it makes.

The day will come when you will be the one under severe attack for serving Him.

The world is going to make fun of you, so be prepared.

The world is going to laugh at you. You might even lose your job for your faith.

When you are born again, filled with the Holy Ghost and start talking in tongues, the world might not want to rub shoulders with you anymore.

They might not want you to sell their product.

You may have to make a decision.

It looked like Job had lost everything. It looked like he had every reason to turn his back on God.

But Job trusted God, and the Bible says, *"So the Lord blessed the latter end of Job more than his beginning: for he had fourteen thousand sheep, and six thousand camels, and a thousand yoke of oxen, and a thousand she asses"* *(Job 42:12).*

Know the Devil's Strategies

When Satan Growls

"'The best evidence of God's presence is the Devil's growl.' So said Mr. C.H. Spurgeon, and that little sentence has helped many a tried and tired child of God to stand fast and even to rejoice under the fiercest attacks of the foe.

"We read in the Book of Samuel that the moment David was crowned at Hebron, 'all the Philistines came up to seek David.' And the moment we get anything from the Lord worth contending for, the Devil comes to seek us."

- A.B. Simpson, in Alliance Weekly

Recipe for Devil's Food

Take one fine boy of tender years,
Remove the ties of love,
Mix with parental neglect
and bad company in equal parts,
Sift in a few foul stores,

121

Add a dash of deviltry,
and a measure of mischief,
All to soak in,
then beat into a fury;
Add a pinch of hate,
then crush with brute force,
putting in a pound of parental cussing;
Shake well,
then turn into the street to harden;
Garnish with ungodliness
Serve with six months in the workhouse.

- Dr. C.H. Williamson

"The thief cometh not, but for to steal, and to kill, and to destroy: I am come that they might have life, and that they might have it more abundantly" (John 10:10).

"Put on the whole armour of God, that ye may be able to stand against the wiles of the devil" (Ephesians 6:11).

"Satan is not original. What he has done to others, he will try to do to you. Satan operates within a very tight job description."

- Pastor Rod Parsley

Professional football teams retain highly paid employees who go to games of opposing teams in order to determine their strengths and weaknesses. The purpose of these scouts is to find out all they can about the game plans of their opponents. They know that if they can find out how an adversary will act and react, they can plan his defeat.

The same is true in the spirit world.

When you know the strategies of Satan, he cannot take you by surprise. When you know there is a spiritual war going on, you will not be vulnerable to the attack of the enemy.

He's a Liar

Adam and Eve were attacked by the devil in the form of a snake; they were deceived by a lie. Satan attacked the family structure of the first family, and as a result, curses fell on Adam and his children (Genesis 3:17).

Look at the basic formula the devil used ... it <u>has not changed since man began walking on the face of the earth!</u>

The devil's formula for destruction is ... L (Lies) + S (Sin) = FD (Family Destruction).

L = Satan lies to entice you to ignore God's will.

S = A sin is committed.

FD = Destruction and curses follow.

The same formula for destruction has been repeated countless millions of times in spiritual history.

L = Cain accepted the lie that his life would be better without Abel.

S = Cain killed Abel (sin).

FD = Cain was damaged and cursed.

"And now art thou cursed from the earth, which hath opened her mouth to receive thy brother's blood from thy hand" *(Genesis 4:11).*

It is vital you understand this.

Throughout spiritual history, the names of the people have changed, but the strategy of the enemy, the formula he uses for destruction, has remained the same ... the devil will use lies and deception to destroy you!

L + S =FD.

Satan lies to the world and makes enticing promises he cannot deliver.

He promises the pregnant teenager tranquility and happiness, a less complicated life if she will just kill the "fetus" inside of her womb.

He promises struggling spouses in a marriage a new and trouble-free life with a new spouse if they will just end their current stress-ridden marriage through a divorce.

He promises confused and frustrated parents they will somehow find relief from their feelings if they just beat and batter their hard-to-control child who is making too much noise in the family living room.

Satan used a lie to remove Adam and Eve from the Garden of Eden, and his strategy has not changed.

"But Peter said, Ananias, why hath Satan filled thine heart to lie to the Holy Ghost, and to keep back part of the price of the land?" (Acts 5:3).

In the days of the apostles, he used a lie to cause Ananias to stumble. It cost Ananias his life.

Today, the devil's strategy is still the same. He will lie to you at every turn, trying to convince you there is something "better" outside the covenant of God.

"If you will just have this one adulterous affair with that gorgeous woman, you will be happy."

"If you do not tithe this month, your bills will be balanced and you can give double next month."

The devil's strategy has not changed!

The best evidence I have that I am healed is because Satan tries to tell me, "You must die — you cannot live."

The best evidence I have that I am accepted by Jesus Christ and the body of Christ is that the devil says, "You do not deserve to be called God's child."

The best evidence I have that I am walking in all of the abundant blessings of God is that the devil declares, "You are cursed. Every bad thing possible happens to you. Life could not get any worse."

A wise saint once said, "The only way you can tell if Satan is lying is if his lips move."

Lying is the number one strategy of the enemy.

There are many today who are still listening to Satan's lies. He tells them "sickness and family problems are from God to teach you a lesson," and they listen.

He tells them, "If you are not healed, it is your fault because you do not have enough faith," and they listen.

He tells them, "You are not good enough to be in God's family," and they listen.

Refuse to listen to anything Satan says! Like water running off a duck's back, you must not entertain what he is saying for even one split second.

Cast those lies out, in the name of Jesus.

The Original Kleptomaniac!

The second strategy you can predict Satan will employ to attack you as a child of God is to try and steal anything he can from you.

If anything has been stolen in your life, Satan is the culprit.

The word translated "thief" in the King James version of the Bible is the Greek word "kleptes". We get the word "kleptomaniac" from this Greek word. The meaning of this word is "a thief by nature" or "a compulsive thief."

The devil is a calculating, deceptive plunderer who moves freely in and out of unsuspecting lives. Every individual living in America has in some way been defrauded or robbed by this indiscriminate thief.

One good thing about identifying Satan as the thief is that God's Word tells us if the thief be caught he must restore what he has taken sevenfold!

"But if he [the thief] be found, he shall restore sevenfold; he shall give all the substance of his house" (Proverbs 6:31).

God is calling for us to bankrupt the kingdom of hell.

Demand that Satan return everything he has taken from you sevenfold!

God has established a law of retribution for you! God has given you power over this thief!

"Behold, I give unto you power to tread on serpents and scorpions, and over all the power of the enemy: and nothing shall by any means hurt you" (Luke 10:19).

The Killer of Joy

The third strategy Satan continues to employ to attack the saints is to kill.

The devil will attempt to kill your friends, your family, your joy, and your soul.

Satan is the mass murderer of the centuries.

From the first animals slain to cover the nakedness of sin to the last of the remnant of Gog and Magog to die in the Apocalypse, Satan is the source of death!

With the inception of sin, death came to be, for the law of God states, *"The wages of sin is [always] death" (Romans 6:23).*

But death need not come for the saints. Christ came to give us power over death.

"Forasmuch then as the children are partakers of flesh and blood, he also himself likewise took part of the same; that through death he might destroy him that had the power of death, that is, the devil" (Hebrews 2:14).

Jesus defeated the grave. It has no victory. He prayed in the garden, "Father, if it by thy will, let this cup pass from me"; and he prayed until his sweat became great drops of blood. And then he died the real death in Gethsemane. He said, "Nevertheless, not what I will, but what thou will, Father." And *"for the joy that was laid before Him, He endured the cross" (Hebrews 12:2).*

God wants His people full of joy — the kind the devil can't steal, that discouragement can't dampen. There's no joy in hell, but in heaven there's joy unspeakable and full of glory.

The Bible says, *"The joy of the Lord is our strength" (Nehemiah 8:10).*

What's standing in the way of your joy? Pain? Infirmity? A rebellious spirit? A lying tongue? Some of you have allowed the devil to walk into your life, steal your joy, steal your anointing, steal your victory ... steal the glory of God right out of your life.

The Corruptive Touch

The fourth and final strategy of Satan is to destroy.

He soils and ruins everything he sees or touches. Contact with the devil means corruption and contamination.

To touch is to taint.

No sinful pleasure can last; it is always just for a season. The end result of all sin must always be destruction.

"For many walk, of whom I have told you often, and now tell you even weeping, that they are the enemies of the cross of Christ: Whose end is destruction, whose God is their belly, and whose glory is in their shame, who mind earthly things" (Philippians 3:18,19).

God has a different end in mind for His children. As you recognize the strategies of Satan, and come against them for yourself and your family, you will win every victory.

"Now thanks be unto God, which always causeth us to triumph in Christ, and maketh manifest the savour of his knowledge by us in every place" (2 Corinthians 2:14).

Receive Local Church Power

Why She Came

"We have in the church of which I am a member, a woman who is very old, very deaf, and whose eyes are bad, but she is always at church, even though she does not hear a word. On Saturday she is given a church bulletin and she looks up and reads the hymns and Scripture lesson. One day she remarked that all she gets out of the service is that received from the bulletin, and I told her what a fine thing it is that she comes. She replied, "Well, you know, the Psalmist said, 'The Lord is in his holy temple, and I come here to meet the Lord.' Of how many who attend church can that be said, I wonder."

- Sunday School Times

"The first banana to leave the bunch is always the first to get peeled."

- Unknown

"Not forsaking the assembling of ourselves together, as the manner of some is; but exhorting one another: and so much the more, as ye see the day approaching" (Hebrews 10:5).

131

"We are in a battlefield, not a recreation room."

- Pastor Rod Parsley

Hebrews 10:5 tells us the power of the corporate anointing makes corporate worship indispensable. One thing that is important to note about this Scripture is that it was written from a first century perspective. These were people who worshiped together almost daily. From that perspective, we are admonished to worship God even more as we see "the day" approaching.

Tommy Hicks, a great man of God, had a vision of the church in the last days. He saw the church as a sleeping giant, bound by the shackles of religious tradition. He saw that the church would begin to wake up, to rise up, and shake off the bondages of the devil.

I do not think the church is awake yet.

We are not yet serious about spiritual survival.

"Many Christians just want to frolic in the flatlands of shallow spiritual experience. They go to church when they feel like it, pay their tithes when they feel like it, read their Bible once in six months (if they have the time), and do not know anything about the Word of God except what someone else tells them.

They come to church and let someone spoon feed them a little bit of spiritual pabulum to them while they go on their merry, fleshly, self-appeasing, self-satisfying, self-indulgent way!

After all, they believe, God will make an exception for them.

The church is not a social club or a place to show off new clothes and flaunt self-indulgent lifestyles. We are in absolute mortal conflict; and whether we realize it or not, we have an adversary who will destroy us unless we stand united through the church.

We are in a battlefield, not a recreation room!

And remember, we are not alone. Our fellow Christians are in the same trenches with us. Each of us must help our brothers and sisters stay on guard.

I am bone of your bone, flesh of your flesh … your body. We must help each other guard against the enemy if we are going to face him.

When a brother falls, do not step on his head! Reach down and pick him up!

He is your brother — ask him if there is anything you can do to help.

How much time have you spent in prayer lifting up the arms of others?

How much time have you spent speaking life into them, asking God to guard their hearts?

We must stop demanding so much more of everyone else than we do of ourselves.

We must spiritually stand with one another. We must look at those around us and say, "I bless you, and ask for God's protection upon your life, in Jesus' name."

"Well, what if they are in sin?"

Sin is God's business, not yours. But if you sense there is difficulty, then pray God will reveal to them the horror of their sin and restore them into communion with Him.

Let us bless and strengthen each other.

Let us stand firmly in the trenches and support each other.

Let us get serious about survival.

Let us guard our hearts, and start to actively love our brothers and sisters in Christ through prayer.

"You have the opportunity to be involved in God's greatest instrument of revival, blessing, healing, salvation, and deliverance of our generation ... the local church."

- Pastor Rod Parsley

The Lord Jesus, our Redeemer, said, *"And I say also unto thee, That thou art Peter, and upon this rock [of revelation] I will build my church; and the gates of hell shall not prevail against it"* (*Matthew 16:18*).

Jesus did not say the gates of hell would not prevail against an evangelistic association or a teaching ministry. He did not say the gates of hell would not prevail against apostolic authority or the prophetic ministry. He said the gates of hell would not prevail against the church!

You say, "Well, He's talking about the universal church." We have a universal God; everything He does is universal in scope. God does have a church which is universal, intangible, and invisible; but that is not what I am referring to. I am referring specifically to the local church God has prepared to give you the power to survive in your daily life.

Some say, "Well I'm saved, so that is all I need. I'm part of the church, and I don't have to belong to any local body or fellowship. Don't put that kind of bondage on me. I just go to church wherever I am led."

On Sunday morning they stick their spiritual radar up to see where they're led. And for the vast majority of them, the only "led" they get is in the bottom of their seat. They're here, they're there, they're everywhere.

These people are "spiritual parasites." They just want to wallow around in the flat lands of shallow spiritual experience, picking up a scrap from the floor here and there that has fallen from the abundant table God sets for His committed people! They don't want commitment; they just want to float along.

When God wants us to see something universal or intangible, He always gives us a tangible representation of that intangible truth. The universal truth of the collective church is mirrored by the tangible representation — the local church that sits on the nearest corner in your neighborhood.

When God wanted us to understand the relationship between our Redeemer and His church, He gave us the marriage covenant. When we look at a man and his wife, we see the relationship between Christ and His church.

Marriage is a covenant, a natural symbol of the universal spiritual union between Christ and His church that is unalterable. That is why in our marriage ceremonies we say "what God joins together, let no man put asunder."

This is the same union He wants between His Son and His church.

Jesus died for every person of every race, every kindred, every tribe, every tongue who has ever walked on this planet, or will ever walk on this planet.

We are all baptized into one body — the universal church. You cannot touch it, you cannot see it, you cannot feel it. It is intangible and it is invisible, but nonetheless it is the church of Jesus Christ.

When Jesus splits the eastern sky, He is going to gather it unto Himself. We are coming off this planet, going extraterrestrial. We will be joined together with the saints from all the ages of time who have ever been or who ever will be after us.

In that hour, we will see the universal church.

But right now, we cannot see it.

So God gives us a natural, physical representation of that which we cannot see ... He calls it the local body. You cannot function in that body with making a commitment.

After Christians came through the charismatic revival, many did not want to commit to a relationship in a local church. The only commitment most people wanted to make to a local church was "I will stay there as long

137

as they bless me. The very moment they do anything I don't like, I am out the door."

Hopefully, you did not make that commitment to your wife. Can you imagine? The first time she burned the toast, you'd throw her out the door!

God is looking for Christians willing to commit to their local church. Your pastor covenants to preach the gospel, to pray for you, to believe God for your miracles. In return, you covenant to commit to the church, to stick by your pastor, and to work together to reach lost souls in your community, in whatever your calling might be.

It is high time in the body of Christ that the people sitting in the pews, and the people in the choir, and the people in the orchestra, and the ushers, and the greeters, and the nursery workers, and the children's ministry workers, and the outreach workers, and the volunteers who sweep the carpet, and the people who work in the offices become as radically faithful to their calling as the people who stand behind that sacred desk.

The Bible says He "set" them in the church. That is the word S-E-T (1 Corinthians 12:28).

When you first pour concrete, it is called "green." If you remove the form from green concrete too soon, it just oozes, without form, all over the ground. But there comes a time when concrete "sets," and the forms can be taken off, leaving the concrete slab to hold the integrity of its own shape.

So, too, in the church.

As you mature in the Lord, the forms can be taken away; your foundation is established. You're committed, you're in the nursery, you're there on Wednesday night. No one has to call you to remind you.

When you are firmly set, someone can come along and kick you, but you don't move. All that will happen is the person doing the kicking will stub their toe!

Everyone is not gifted to be an apostle, a prophet, an evangelist, a pastor, or a teacher. Everyone does not have the gift of working of miracles or the gifts of healing.

But there is one ministry that everyone has ... the ministry of a servant. And in your local church body, it is vital you serve whenever possible.

Rev. W.B. Godbey defined it this way: "Oh! The infinite value of the humble gospel helpers. Thousands of people who have no gifts as leaders but who are number one helpers. How grand revival work moves along when red hot platoons of fire-baptized helpers crowd around God's heroic leaders of the embattled hosts!"

Brother, this is a warfare, and we need every single, solitary person ready and able to defend their battle station.

Maybe your gifting is prayer.

Maybe your gifting is giving.

Maybe your gifting is ushering.

Maybe your gifting is taking care of the babies in the nursery and ministering to the future generation that is going to herald in the second coming of Jesus Christ.

It is time we start coming into the church doors with a "let me bless you" attitude instead of a "bless me" attitude. "How can I help you? What can I do for you? Lord, I'm here to serve you. Show me my place, and I'll get in it. I'll go to work, and I'll be faithful."

It's time to get faithful. It is time to wake up and shake yourself, and commit to your local church.

You need to wake up, stir yourself, and realize this is a spiritual conflict. If you are to be a warrior in God's kingdom, you need to be spiritually prepared by partaking in all the ministries available to you through the church assembly!

"How dare you run around thinking everything's supposed to pop up posies because you were in praise and worship for fifteen minutes? All you've done is jerked on the devil's chain!"

- Pastor Rod Parsley

We are invading enemy-held territory with all the arsenal of God at our disposal. Yet, while some are brandishing swords and spears, others are waving around butter knifes.

Instead of carrying spiritual machine guns, many Christians are going into battle with squirt guns.

You do not have the ammunition.

You do not have the combustion — the anointing.

The anointing does not come free. You do not get it by watching television, or by going about your business at work. You get the anointing in the presence of God, on your face with the Word open!

"Well, I wish I had the anointing."

No, you don't.

You claim to want it, but the only time you are willing to invest to receive it is the two hours you spend at church on Sunday morning. You want the victory without ever going into battle.

It is time to depart from nursery school mentality and realize we are in the middle of a vicious spiritual war!

How dare you run around thinking everything's supposed to pop up posies because you were in praise and worship for fifteen minutes? All you've done is jerked on the devil's chain!

This is spiritual life and death. It is not playing around; it is not take it or leave it. Your life depends on this.

Diligently Guard Your Family

It Interfered With His Prayers

"There was once an old codfish dealer, a very earnest and sincere man, who lived prayerfully every day. One of the great joys of his life was the family worship hour. One year, two other merchants persuaded him to go into a deal with them by which they could control all the codfish in the market and greatly increase the price. The plan was succeeding well, when this good man learned that many poor people in Boston were suffering because of the great advance in the price of codfish. It troubled him so that he broke down in trying to pray at the family altar, and he went straight to the men who had led him into the plot and told them that he could not go on with it.

"Said the old man: 'I cannot afford to do anything which interferes with my family prayers. And this morning when I got down on my knees and tried to pray, there was a mountain of codfish before me high enough to shut out the throne of God, and I could not pray. I tried my best to get around it or over it, but every time I started to pray that codfish loomed up between me and my God. I will not have my family prayers spoiled for all the codfish in the Atlantic Ocean. And I shall have nothing to do with this market control business, or with any money made from it.'"

— Pentecostal Evangel

"Children, Obey your parents in the Lord [as His representatives], for this is just and right. Honor (esteem and value as precious) your father and your mother — this is the first commandment with a promise — That all may be well with you and that you may live long on the earth" (Ephesians 6:1-3, AMP).

"Wives, be subject (be submissive and adapt yourselves) to your own husbands as [a service] to the Lord. For the husband is head of the wife as Christ is the Head of the church, Himself the Savior of [His] body. As the church is subject to Christ, so let wives also be subject in everything to their husbands. Husbands, love your wives, as Christ loved the church and gave Himself up for her, So that He might sanctify her, having cleansed her by the washing of water with the Word, That He might present the church to Himself in glorious splendor, without spot or wrinkle or any such things [that she might be

holy and faultless]. Even so husbands should love their wives as [being in a sense] their own bodies. He who loves his own wife loves himself. For no man ever hated his own flesh, but nourishes and carefully protects and cherishes it, as Christ does the church" (Ephesians 5:22-29, AMP).

"A gentle nudging of the Holy Ghost to pray, a split second of time, might make the difference between life and death."

- Pastor Rod Parsley

The greatest asset today's family has is the leading of the Holy Ghost. We must learn to discern the prophetic voice of God. It is time to open our spiritual ears to the gentle wooing of the Holy Ghost, to learn to obey, to wake up and get serious.

We are living in the last days!

A gentle nudging of the Holy Ghost to pray, a split second of time, might make the difference between life and death in your family. It may be just a gentle "No, do not go to the store right now; just worship me a little while." And while you are worshiping Him, the devil's plan to meet you head-on with a truck is thwarted because you heard — and obeyed — when God said, "Just worship me a little while."

This is a survival strategy for the last days. There is an adversary who wants your family dead ... D-E-A-D. He wants you out of the way; he wants you silenced. He will do anything he can do to stop you, because you are shaking his kingdom.

Satan hates a godly family because he knows its spiritual strength. If Satan has his way, you will be walking around divorced this time next year. If Satan has his way, he will send you spinning into bankruptcy this time next year.

The devil is causing families to become so caught up with obtaining worldly possessions they no longer have time to pray, read the Word, or worship together as a family.

Evil forces are attacking the finances in many families until the parents are forced to work long hours. There is little or no time left for parents to spend with their children, or with each other. Communication lines are being cut off. Many times they become so exhausted they are too tired to pray, and often stop going to church.

Dads, if you have not prayed with your family in the last fifteen years ... start today. Bless the food at the next meal, and then teach your children how to bless the food at future meals.

How much different family life would be if before any person in the household left home for the day everyone would join together in the living room, hold hands, unite together, and pray a hedge of protection around the entire family unit!

This is no time for us to sit back whining and complaining about what Satan is doing to attack and destroy our families and loved ones ... it is time to fight!

This is no time for us to sit back in fear ... wondering, waiting to see how Satan is going to attack our family next. It is time for Christian families to take the power and authority God has given to us and use it against the enemy!

As the children of Israel were preparing to enter their promised land, they were not only commanded to obey all the commandments of the covenant, but they were also commanded to remember all the great and mighty miracles God had done for them and to teach them to their children.

Moses said, *"Only take heed, and guard your life diligently, lest you forget the things which your eyes have seen and lest they depart from your [mind and] heart all the days of your life. Teach them to your children, and your children's children — Especially how on the day that you stood before the Lord your God in Horeb, the Lord said to me, Gather the people together to Me, and I will make them hear My words, that they may learn [reverently] to fear Me all the days they live upon the earth and that they may teach their children"* (Deuteronomy 4:9,10 AMP).

It is time for us to get our houses in order and teach our children about the mighty miracles of our loving God if we are going to survive in these last days! The spiritual strength of the church today depends upon the spiritual strength of its families.

Satan's strategy since Adam and Eve has been to tear down and destroy the spiritual foundation in the home. We must teach our children how to recognize and thwart the actions of the enemy.

Proverbs 22:6 tells us to *"Train up a child in the way he should go: and when he is old, he will not depart from it."*

In many homes, the Word of God has been replaced by television. The Bible is never even opened or read together as a family. It has been cast aside, neglected, and almost forgotten.

It is time to reestablish the home as the spiritual foundation God intended it to be. Parents and grandparents must rise up in the spirit and make a new commitment to God that says, *"As for me and my house, we will serve the Lord" (Joshua 24:15).*

Men, it is time for you to take the position God has given you as head of your household. Accept your responsibility. Cover your family in prayer. Teach and train your children about God and His Word. It is not the responsibility of the church to teach your children about God ... it is primarily your job. The church is there to supplement the teaching and training your children receive at home. Work as a team with your wife to teach and nurture your children.

Women, if you are a single parent, or if your husband is unsaved or unwilling to accept his responsibility for the spiritual condition of your family, accept this as your responsibility. Establish your home as a spiritual training ground for your children. God will honor you, and will anoint and strengthen you.

Parents, determine now, regardless of the cost, no matter what battles you might face, that you and your family will serve and obey God.

Get Set in the Church

Constrained by Love

A Hindu convert was once asked if, for a certain salary, he was willing to go and try to commence a mission in a neighboring district where he would be sure to meet with great difficulties, and perhaps be persecuted and put to death. "I cannot do it for money," he replied, "but I can do it for Christ," and he went. "The love of Christ constraineth" (2 Corinthians 5:14).

- Glad Tidings

"But now are they many members, yet but one body ... And God hath set some in the church, first apostles, secondarily prophets, thirdly teachers, after that miracles, then gifts of healings, helps, governments, diversities of tongues" (2 Corinthians 12:20,28).

"If you are called and equipped as a farmer, leave lion taming alone. The reason for such falling away in the ranks of God is that too many people are operating outside their calling."

- Pastor Rod Parsley

Another serious survival strategy is to find your place and get set.

"The gifts and calling of God are without repentance" (Romans 11:29).

What has God called you to do?

The anointing follows the calling.

If you are not anointed to do a given work, stay away from it. Otherwise, you will find yourself working in the flesh, and your ability will be limited to your own strength. In your own ability and strength, the devil will defeat you every single time.

Find your place and fill it.

No task God has called you to do is demeaning.

Not everyone is not called to preach or to prophesy. The ministry of helps is a vital function in the body of Christ. Many are called to be armor bearers (see 1 Samuel 14:1).

"And David came to Saul, and stood before him: and he loved him greatly; and he became his armourbearer" (1 Samuel 16:21).

The function of an armor bearer in Bible times was to hold the shield and carry the sword.

Ephesians 6 stresses the importance of our armor. Verse 16 states, *"Above all, taking the shield of faith, wherewith ye shall be able to quench all the fiery darts of the wicked."*

Everyone is responsible for their own personal faith, but that corporate shield of faith is held up by armor bearers. If they do not show up, no matter how strong the leader's personal faith may be, the leader will be naked ... without corporate faith, and the ministry will be subject to the fiery darts of the enemy.

God is calling each of us to intercede ... to trevail ... to mourn, to be armor bearers for His church. He needs us to stand in the gap for lost souls in our communities, nation and world, and for the body of Christ.

"And I sought a man among them who should build up the wall and stand in the gap before Me for the land, that I should not destroy it, but I found none. Therefore have I poured out My indignation upon them; I have consumed them with the fire of My wrath; their own way have I repaid [by bringing it] upon their own heads, says the Lord God" (Ezekiel 22:30,31 AMP).

The Day of the Lord is drawing near. Judgment, such as the world has never known, is coming upon this earth — and God is looking for spiritual warriors who will stand in the gap for individuals, and for His church.

Just as Jesus made intercession for the world through His life and death, and has reconciled us to God, we have been given the ministry of reconciliation for the church:

"And all things are of God, who hath reconciled us to himself by Jesus Christ, and hath given to us the ministry of reconciliation; To wit, that God was in Christ, reconciling the world unto himself, not imputing their trespasses unto them; and hath committed unto us the word of reconciliation. Now then we are ambassadors for Christ, as though God did beseech you by us: we pray you in Christ's stead, be ye reconciled to God" (2 Corinthians 5:18-20).

One tangible way to set yourself in the church, the body of Christ, is to become an intercessor. Be a need-meeter. Allow God to flow through your life in prayer, and through your actions.

Cry out to God on behalf of the lost around you. Enter into the bowels of intercession for the sin and corruption around you. Cry out to God for His mercy.

This is one way to undergird yourself and survive in this perilous time.

"When the trials of your faith come, and you feel like bowing down under their weight, remember the three Hebrew children and the fiery furnace. They did not bow, and they did not burn."

- Pastor Rod Parsley

Shadrach, Meshach, and Abednego declared, in the face of certain destruction, that they would continue to serve the Lord God. While everyone around them bowed to King Nebuchadnezzar and worshiped him, they stood straight and worshiped God ... they were SET in the ways of their God.

"And the princes, governors, and captains, and the king's counsellors, being gathered together, saw these men, upon whose bodies the fire had no power, nor was an hair of their head singed, neither were their coats changed, nor the smell of fire had passed on them" (Daniel 3:27).

We may be battered, but we are not bowed.

We are set in the ways of God and His church (Psalm 119).

I am more determined than ever to grasp hold of the hands of those who are in the foxhole with me.

We must find our place and fill it.

I need you, as members of the body of Christ — no matter who you are or where you are — to pray for me, just as I will pray for you.

155

Like Aaron and Hur, helpers/armor bearers must lift up the hands of God's leaders.

Only then can the victory of the corporate church be won.

I am determined to point my finger in the devil's face and command him to take his hands off you, and off the church.

I am determined for the blessings of God to be released in your life.

Learn to look beyond the fiery furnace.

It is time we allowed God to take us through the furnace, through the trial, and through the tribulation. When He brings us out on the other side, and we do not even smell like smoke, we will proclaim for all to hear: "There is a God in Israel who is able to deliver."

Place your confidence and trust in the delivering power of God to bring you through. Whenever you are going through, remember, like Shadrach, Meshach and Abednego, you are just going through!

As you and I become stronger, then we can pray for others, making the entire body of Christ and His church a unified, strong body of believers who are determined not to just resist the enemy, but to absolutely destroy him!

The Day of the Lord is coming — when Christ will return and judgment will come upon the earth.

As you and I become SET in the church, and accept our spiritual responsibilities, God will empower us to turn entire nations around for His glory.

It is God's plan and purpose to use us to save untold thousands from the destruction that is coming.

Can you hear it?

By His Spirit, God is sounding an alarm. He is looking for men and women who, like Shadrach, Meshach and Abednego, will walk through the fiery furnace on behalf of lost souls.

The church is about to experience a great outpouring of the Holy Spirit, greater than anything the world has ever seen.

God is going to restore all Satan has stolen from the church of Jesus Christ.

The Holy Spirit is going to be poured out upon all flesh.

Pray Always

All Traced to Kneeling Figures!

"Every great movement of God can be traced to a kneeling figure! Therefore, *'Ye that make mention of the Lord, KEEP NOT SILENCE' (Isaiah 6:6b)."*

- D.L. Moody

"Praying always with all prayer and supplication in the Spirit, and watching thereunto with all perseverance and supplication for all saints" (Ephesians 6:18).

"Prayer of intercession is urgent prayer in known or unknown tongues for divine intervention on behalf of a pressing need."
- Pastor Rod Parsley

There are six basic kinds of prayer, and all six need to be active in your life if you are to survive unsurvivable times:

A.) The Prayer of Agreement

"Again I say unto you, That if two of you shall agree on earth as touching any thing that they shall ask, it shall be done for them of my Father which is in heaven" (Matthew 18:19).

Having a prayer partner who can come into agreement with you in prayer greatly multiplies your effectiveness. The best possible agreement is between a godly husband and wife.

B.) The Prayer of Faith

"The prayer of faith shall save the sick" (James 5:15).

The prayer of faith will move any mountain. To pray the prayer of faith, it is necessary for one to first have faith. Faith is built on God's Word and our relation to the Word and to God.

Dr. Lester Sumrall puts it this way: Faith is simply knowing God.

C.) The Prayer of Consecration

The prayer of consecration sets something or someone apart to God's exclusive service.

"Having therefore, brethren, boldness to enter into the holiest by the blood of Jesus, By a new and living way, which he hath consecrated for us, through the veil, that is to say, his flesh" *(Hebrews 10:12-20).*

D.) <u>The Prayer of Thanksgiving</u>

The prayer of thanksgiving gives praise for what God has done.

"Be careful for nothing; but in every thing by prayer and supplication with thanksgiving let your requests be made known unto God" *(Philippians 4:6).*

E.) <u>Prayer in the Spirit</u>

Prayer in the Spirit is exactly that — prayer in a language that comes from the Spirit of God and not from our own understanding.

"For he that speaketh in an unknown tongue speaketh not unto men, but unto God: for no man understandeth him; howbeit in the spirit he speaketh mysteries" *(1 Corinthians 14:2).*

F.) <u>Prayer of Intercession</u>

The prayer of intercession is urgent prayer in known or unknown tongues that intercedes for divine intervention on behalf of a pressing need for another.

"Wherefore he is able also to save them to the uttermost that come unto God by him, seeing he ever liveth to make intercession for them" *(Hebrews 7:25).*

As our intercessor, Jesus identified with man. He did not elevate Himself above us, but humbled Himself and was made in the likeness of men.

In identifying with us, He was willing to lay down His divine attributes and become like us … sharing the same human nature and being made like us in all respects (Philippians 2:7,8).

"Forasmuch then as the children are partakers of flesh and blood, he also himself likewise took part of the same; that through death he might destroy him that had the power of death, that is, the devil … For verily he took not on him the nature of angels; but he took on him the seed of Abraham. Wherefore in all things it behooved him to be made like unto his brethren, that he might be a merciful and faithful high priest in things pertaining to God, to make reconciliation for the sins of the people" (Hebrews 2:14,16,17).

"In the heat of the conflict, you cannot afford to be out of touch with your Commander-in-Chief."

- Pastor Rod Parsley

Prayer is our communication link with the Lord.

The plan of God is this: He wants you to stay within calling distance.

If you are out of touch, you experience a breakdown in the lines of communication from headquarters. When that happens, you become motivated and manipulated by that little bunch of grey matter inside your bony skull, called the brain.

When communication is cut off from God, you are motivated by your own deceived flesh; your ears are deaf to the sweet, soft voice of the living Creator.

Wise up and wake up!

You have an adversary, and he will kill you with a hangnail if you will let him. In the heat of the conflict, you cannot afford to be out of touch with your Commander-in-Chief.

The young man who leads us to the throne of God in praise and worship at World Harvest Church would not be alive today if he had not heard and obeyed that still, small voice.

I believe with all my heart if we will learn to recognize the small inward witness of the Holy

Ghost, we will be able to avoid and avert many of the schemes of the devil.

You will learn to recognize that voice through communication with God, through prayer.

When you begin to pray, you have access into the spirit realm — where God is — and He will begin to reveal to you the root causes of the battles you are facing.

Your battle is not against the sickness ... arthritis ... diabetes ... heart condition ... hearing loss ... or any other disease the enemy has put upon your body.

Your battle is not with your husband ... wife ... children or any other family member.

Your battle is not with your boss or your fellow employees.

Your battle is not with your financial condition ... your lack of finances ... overdue bills.

Your warfare is not on the surface. It is not in the circumstances as you see them. Your warfare is not in the natural world that is governed by your five natural senses. Your battle is in the spirit realm.

Wake up and recognize behind the circumstances you are facing there are spiritual powers and rulers of darkness at work.

Behind the political struggles ... communism ... racial prejudice ... crime ... violence ... economic conditions ... in the nations of the earth, there are evil forces at work.

There are spirits of confusion, fear, frustration, promiscuity, homosexuality, lust, envy, jealousy, hatred, violence, rebellion, murder, suicide, resentment, selfishness and many others at work to kill, steal and destroy.

Before you can tear down the strongholds the enemy has built in your home, city and nation, you must first know the enemy — the spirit forces that are the root cause of your circumstances. When a soldier is being attacked on every side, he cannot defend himself without weapons.

The only way to have the sharp spiritual eyes necessary to know and recognize the enemy, the only way to defend against the enemy once we recognize his evil works — is through PRAYER!

Without prayer, you are like a blindfolded soldier without a weapon — unable to see the enemy, and without the firepower to destroy him.

Just as God anointed Jesus with the Holy Spirit and gave Him power and authority to destroy the works of the devil, He has given us power and authority over all the power of the enemy (Luke 10:19).

He has given us the authority to bind and loose:

"Whatsoever ye shall bind on earth shall be bound in heaven: and whatsoever ye shall loose on earth shall be loosed in heaven" (Matthew 18:18).

The spiritual key to releasing that power and authority is PRAYER.

To survive these perilous times, the battle must first be won on your face before God ... interceding, weeping, travailing — battling the forces of darkness with the mighty weapon of prayer.

Guard Your Heart

"Only take heed to thyself, and keep thy soul diligently, lest thou forget the things which thine eyes have seen, and lest they depart from thy heart all the days of thy life: but teach them thy sons, and thy sons' sons" (Deuteronomy 4:9).

"Let your heart therefore be perfect with the Lord our God, to walk in his statutes, and to keep his commandments, as at this day" (1 Kings 8:61).

And if thou wilt walk before me, as David thy father walked, in integrity of heart, and in uprightness, to do according to all that I have commanded thee, and wilt keep my statutes and my judgments" (1 Kings 9:4).

"Blessed are they that keep his testimonies, and that seek him with the whole heart" (Psalm 119:2).

"He taught me also, and said unto me, Let thine heart retain my words: keep my commandments, and live" (Proverb 4:4).

"We must place a guard on our hearts and exercise extreme care over what we let in."

- Pastor Rod Parsley

Guard your heart ... it must have but one king.

"Keep thy heart with all diligence; for out of it are the issues of life" (Proverb 4:23).

The word "keep" in this passage means "to set armed guards around."

Be careful what your eyes see, what your ears hear.

Be careful of the company you keep.

Guard yourself against evil ideas and the people who express them to you.

Cut the umbilical cord from the world and get hooked up to the biblical cord.

Set armed guards around your camp and guard your heart at all cost! Give no place to the devil.

There is only one way for the devil to get a place in your heart — you have to give it to him. Clint Brown wrote a song that says:

"Satan, don't be deceived — you're not getting by
When His army intercedes — you're identified
Stand back you spirits of darkness
Stay out of this dwelling place
We will war against all evil with praise."

Ephesians 4:7 says, *"Neither give place to the devil."* The word "place" comes from a very interesting Greek word, "topos." It means several different things, including "a position of opportunity."

Never give the devil a position of opportunity — such as sin — to enter your life.

"Remember therefore from whence thou art fallen, and repent, and do the first works; or else I will come unto thee quickly, and will remove thy candlestick out of his place, except thou repent" (Revelation 2:5).

In the above scripture, God is speaking to the church at Ephesus, and He is saying to them, "If you do not repent, if you do not guard your heart against sin, I will come and remove your candlestick out of its place. I will move your church out of its position of opportunity."

God gives every person and every church a position of opportunity.

In Ephesians 4:7, God is also saying, "Do not give the devil any position of opportunity." Why?

Because he will seize on that opportunity and bring you down into the eternal death of hell if you let him.

We guard our hearts and enter the realm of the spirit by denying the devil access into our spiritual affairs. Do not wait until the devil moves in and unpacks his suitcase of blight and discouragement to kick him out.

Do not wait until he unpacks his distress and unloads a big accident in your family to scream out to God, "Help us get rid of the devil!"

It is much easier to head the devil off at the pass.

Guard your heart to survive.

Exalt God

A.P. Gibbs correctly observed that ministry is "that which comes down from the Father, by the Son, in the power of the Spirit, through the human instrument and goes up by the power of the Holy Spirit, through the Son, to the Father."

- A.P. Gibbs, Worship

"But they that wait upon the Lord shall renew their strength; they shall mount up with wings as eagles; they shall run, and not be weary; and they shall walk, and not faint" (Isaiah 40:31).

"Complacency is a sickening cancer eating away at the power of the New Testament church."

- Pastor Rod Parsley

"And it shall come to pass afterward, that I will pour out my spirit upon all flesh; and your sons and your daughters shall prophesy, your old men shall dream dreams, your young men shall see visions: And also upon the servants and upon the handmaids in those days will I pour out my spirit" (Joel 2:28,29).

Joel prophesied that revival was coming!

Holiness, prayer, praise, and worship bring revival.

Peter stood up on the day of Pentecost and said the revival Joel had prophesied had begun.

"For these are not drunken, as ye suppose, seeing it is but the third hour of the day. But this is that which was spoken by the prophet Joel;" (Acts 2:15,16).

Revival started this age, and this age will end with even greater revival. The revival that is coming on the earth will make every other revival the world has ever known look like a Sunday school picnic. An unprecedented outpouring of the glory of God is about to fall on this earth!

We are in the beginnings of the last great end-time revival, and the church needs to wake up and see what God is doing in the earth.

Walls are falling down, and people are hearing the Gospel who have never heard it before.

Revival is moving across this land, and we will never be the same. When there is revival, saints get right with God.

When there is revival, the power of God is in manifestation. Praise and worship are two key spiritual ingredients to release revival.

"Thou shalt worship the Lord thy God, and him only shalt thou serve" (Luke 4:8).

Worship is part of our service to God, and keeps us in an attitude of reverence.

"And again, Praise the Lord ... and laud him, all ye people" (Romans 15:11).

Praise and worship draw us close to God, and help us to better know His will for our lives. Under the New Covenant, praise is our sacrifice — replacing the perfect lamb and other sacrifices of the Old Law.

"By him therefore let us offer the sacrifice of praise to God continually, that is, the fruit of our lips giving thanks to his name" (Hebrews 13:15).

Under the old law, the people were told to bring the firstfruits of their labors in the field to

God. Under the new covenant, we are asked to bring the *"fruit of our lips"* as a sacrifice to our heavenly Father.

We are encouraged to praise God in everything we do.

"Praise ye the Lord. Praise God in his sanctuary: praise him in the firmament of his power.

Praise him for his mighty acts: praise him according to his excellent greatness.

Praise him with the sound of the trumpet: praise him with the psaltery and harp.

Praise him with the timbrel and dance: praise him with stringed instruments and organs.

Praise him upon the loud cymbals: praise him upon the high sounding cymbals.

Let every thing that hath breath praise the Lord. Praise ye the Lord" (Psalm 150).

"I believe there are people today who want life. They are tired of the doldrums and drudgery of yesterday, and they want fresh oil."
- Pastor Rod Parsley

"Then took Mary a pound of ointment of spikenard, very costly, and anointed the feet of Jesus, and wiped his feet with her hair: and the house was filled with the odour of the ointment" *(John 12:3).*

True worship is placing our whole lives — all we deem valuable — at the feet of Jesus. So much will be accomplished in our lives if we follow the pattern Mary employed. If we submit to the lordship of Jesus, then we will open new vistas of worship and power far greater than we ever dreamed.

Jesus said, *"It is the spirit that quickeneth; the flesh profiteth nothing: the words that I speak unto you, they are spirit, and they are life"* *(John 6:63).*

I believe there are people today who want life. They are tired of the doldrums and drudgery of yesterday, and they want fresh oil. They want a new life, a new beginning, a new vision, a new strength. They want a new ability, a new anointing, and a new fervency in God.

When we achieve this, we will make the devil angry. He thinks he has the church lulled to sleep, but every time he has the church at this point, we prove him wrong.

My Dad used to pride himself on being able to keep a fire going. I have seen the character of my Heavenly Father many times in my natural father. Every night my Dad would bank our fire. When the time came to go to bed, he would scoop up all the day's ashes and pile them on top of the fire.

I would say, "Dad, why are you doing that? Why don't you just let it burn out?"

He would say, "No, I am preserving it."

He would take those ashes and pack them down on top of the fire; without oxygen, the fire would smoulder into a heap of grayness.

Skeptics may think the church is just a lump of gray and lifeless matter from yesterday — that it is not burning and glowing.

But I have news for them!

In the morning when my Dad climbed out of bed, he would start to fan away those ashes on top of the heap. He would begin to blow on the coals underneath, and ignited by the oxygen of his breath, the embers from yesterday's fire burst into flame!

The Bible says, *"And they that shall be of thee shall build the old waste places: thou shalt raise up the foundations of many generations; and thou shalt be called, The repairer of the breach, The restorer of paths to dwell in" (Isaiah 58:12).*

We are going to take yesterday's fire and let the Holy Ghost fan it. God is going to rekindle the new blaze burning in the church of Jesus Christ, and this new generation shall go forth to repair the breach the devil has created between God and the people.

God's remnant people will praise Him militantly.

They will praise Him wildly and exuberantly.

It is time for the church to come alive.

Let the breath of God breathe on you.

Start talking about the love of Jesus and the power of the Holy Ghost. Lose sight of men and start proclaiming the majesty of Jesus; start extolling and magnifying His name.

It is a new day.

There are changes going on in the body of Christ. Paul said, *"While we look not at the things which are seen, but at the things which are not seen: for the things which are seen are temporal; but the things which are not seen are eternal" (2 Corinthians 4:18).*

"Temporal" means "subject to change." God is changing; God is moving on the church.

There are some men of God who are being raised up in this hour with the same stature as a

Martin Luther, with the same fervency of a John Wesley, with the same power of one named John who came out of the wilderness eating locusts and wild honey, declaring, *"Repent ye: for the kingdom of heaven is at hand" (Matthew 3:2).*

There are some people being raised up in this hour with the fervency of Jesus. I fully believe we are the generation that is destined to usher in the coming of the Lord.

We are His heralds, His prophets.

God is raising up some people who, like John the Baptist, are saying, *"He must increase, but I must decrease" (John 3:30).*

God is raising up some men and women who would just as soon preach behind a curtain as before the multiplied millions. God is raising up some powerful men ... not only in the pulpit, but in the pew.

God is raising up some families who are going to herald the coming of the Lord in the corridors of the local school, in the grocery store, in the neighborhood park.

They are going to prophetically declare in the realm of the spirit, *"Behold, the Lamb of God, which taketh away the sin of the world" (John 1:29).*

It is a new hour.

There are some new and different characteristics of this move of God.

Complacency is a sickening cancer eating away at the power of the New Testament church. "Let someone else do it. Let someone else pray. Let someone else witness. Let someone else storm the gates of hell. I will sit here in my padded pew and raise my hands once a week."

Help us, God, to stir up the gift that is within us.

We have a heritage in the Lord, an inheritance of the saints. We have been given some coals from the altar of God that are burning and glowing, and God has placed them on the inside of us. And now, He is breathing Holy Spirit oxygen upon us to fan a flame through praise and worship that will cause revival to spread to the four corners of the earth. Our generation has never seen this kind of revival.

It is time to go forward, to do more than we have ever done before.

It is time to pray without ceasing, to witness with a fervency only the Holy Ghost can give, to praise and worship our God with every fiber of our being so men and women will be convicted of their sins by the glory of the presence of Jesus Christ upon our lives.

It is war time — time for battle.

Praise and worship are mighty weapons of war.

Nehemiah had never seen revival in his generation. He had only heard there used to be a flame in Jerusalem, and the hand of Yahweh delivered His people — His right arm brought them great victory. But Nehemiah did not know anything about it, just like this generation does not know anything about real revival.

We do not know what revival is like, nor do we sometimes appear to care what it would be like if a new and mighty revival, ushered in by the breath of God, would explode upon our dying world.

We do not understand. We have only heard about it, and some of us have not even cared to hear about it. We do not know what it is like to come two hours early to a service because sinners are packing out the church, crying out and searching for God.

I am talking about revival breathed by the oxygen of the Spirit of God, fanned by our praise and worship.

We are going to be set ablaze through praise and worship or stagnate in sin.

Fear Nothing But God

Stopped by a Smile

"Miss C. Lefinwell, a missionary in China, gave the following account of deliverance from death by the Boxers: "There was a lady missionary whom the Boxers told to kneel down as they prepared to cut off her head. She knelt as told, but as she did so, she looked up into the man's face and actually smiled. As she looked at him a moment, thus smiling, it seemed as if his face began to change and to reflect the smile. He stepped back a little, and then continued to withdraw, together with his companions, until after a little they all fled, leaving the lady alone.

"As the Boxers were retreating the leader turned and said to her: 'You cannot die. You are immortal.' If her face had shown fear, they would have killed her without hesitation. I suppose the smile seemed supernatural. She afterward said, 'I did not know that I smiled.'"

- Life of Missionary

"Fear thou not; for I am with thee: be not dismayed; for I am thy God: I will strengthen thee; yea, I will help thee; yea, I will uphold thee with the right hand of my righteousness" (Isaiah 41:10).

> *"The Bible said in the last days men's hearts will fail them for fear. But do not hang your head down or wring your hands, because He was not talking about you."*
>
> *- Pastor Rod Parsley*

I do not have a spirit of fear.

"For God hath not given us the spirit of fear; but of power, and of love, and of a sound mind" (2 Timothy 1:7).

If you have a spirit of fear, you did not acquire it from God, because He said, *"Fear thou not; for I am with thee: be not dismayed; for I am thy God: I will strengthen thee; yea, I will help thee; yea, I will uphold thee with the right hand of my righteousness" (Isaiah 41:10).*

Be not dismayed.

"But, Pastor Rod, you do not know what is going on at my house."

Be not dismayed.

Jesus said, *"Let not your heart be troubled: ye believe in God, believe in me. In my Father's house are many mansions: if it were not so, I would have told you. I go to prepare a place for you" (John 14:1-3).*

Fear not.

The Bible said in the last days men's hearts will fail them for fear.

"Men's hearts failing them for fear, and for looking after those things which are coming on

the earth: for the powers of heaven shall be shaken" (Luke 21:26).

Nations will collapse; economies will come apart at the seams; you will see turmoil, trouble, strife, hunger, famine, pestilence, earthquakes, and rumors of wars.

"And ye shall hear of wars and rumours of wars: see that ye be not troubled: for all these things must come to pass, but the end is not yet. For nation shall rise against nation, and kingdom against kingdom: and there shall be famines, and pestilences, and earthquakes, in divers places. All these are the beginning of sorrows" (Matthew 24:6-8).

God said in the last days it is going to get horrific. Everyday life will be more frightening than a horror movie. It will take a bag of gold to buy a piece of bread. Epidemics like AIDS will sweep the continents.

Today, when someone gets a little mole on their face, the devil screams his lie: "Cancer! Your grandmother died of it, and now it is going to get you, too."

My grandfather was taking an aspirin one night, and my father said, "Well, Dad, do you have a headache?"

"No," he replied, "I am taking this in case I get one."

Don't laugh; you do the same thing. You go to the drug store, and you need a grocery cart to carry out your economy size bottle of aspirin. You are planning a headache.

People are fearful.

Nearly one marriage in two ends in divorce; children are growing up without parents; twelve year-olds and thirteen year-olds are having babies. Kids are shooting up dope; machine guns are in the hands of teenagers on crack cocaine. Sexually transmitted diseases are up 75 percent since 1960.

It is scary out there.

We put our money in bags with holes in them; we put our financial security in banks ... and they collapse.

The Bible said in the last days men's hearts will fail them for fear (Luke 21:26). But don't hang your head down or wring your hands, because He was not talking about you.

The same Bible that said men's hearts would fail them for fear also says "fear not."

"But even the very hairs of your head are all numbered. Fear not therefore: ye are of more value than many sparrows" (Luke 12:7).

Why should we be free from fear?

Because Jesus said *"I am with you alway, even unto the end of the world. Amen" (Matthew 28:20).*

In Jeremiah, God said, *"Be not afraid of their faces: for I am with thee to deliver thee, saith the Lord. Then the Lord put forth his hand, and touched my mouth. And the Lord said unto me, Behold, I have put my words in thy mouth. See, I have this day set thee over the nations and over the kingdoms, to root out, and to pull down, and to destroy, and to throw down, to build, and to plant"* (Jeremiah 1:8-10).

Do not be troubled or dismayed — be bold! You have the power to rule over kingdoms and to root out and destroy the enemy!

"The wicked flee when no man pursueth" (Proverbs 28:1a).

The wicked flee in fear when nothing pursues them but an illusion and an empty lie! The devil presents them with an opportunity to fear.

Do you know what fear is?

False Evidence that Appears Real.

It is a lie, an illusion. Fear is the counterfeit of faith. They are mutually exclusive and cancel one another out. They cannot live in the same heart.

Be full of faith, not full of fear. *"The righteous are bold as a lion"* (Proverbs 8:1b). As you trust in God, you will become bold in His strength.

Fear thou not, for God is with you!

In Psalms, it says, *"The Lord is my shepherd; I shall not want" (Psalm 23:1).*

Let the economies collapse; if it takes a bag of gold to buy a slice of bread, we will own the bakery.

Do not trouble your heart.

What happens tomorrow will not surprise or astound Jesus. He wrote the book. He said, "In the last days men will run to and fro like a bunch of ants on an anthill, running everywhere and nowhere."

Men's hearts will fail them because they are full of fear. They will fear for their children's lives; they will fear for their own lives.

Job said, *"And unto man he said, Behold, the fear of the Lord, that is wisdom; and to depart from evil is understanding" (Job 28:28).*

The fear of the Lord is a healthy fear, since it is the beginning of wisdom, but you need not fear the empty lies of the devil.

Whom shall I fear? For what shall men do to me?

"The Lord is my shepherd; I shall not want. He maketh me to lie down in green pastures: he leadeth me beside the still waters. He restoreth my soul: he leadeth me in the paths of righteousness for his name's sake. Yea, though I walk through the valley of the shadow of death,

I will fear no evil: for thou art with me; thy rod and thy staff they comfort me" (Psalm 23:1-4).

Did you think He had a shepherd's rod because He was so old He could hardly get around?

He has that rod because it is a weapon against predators.

My Heavenly Father is my shepherd. His rod and His staff comfort and protect me. Tomorrow will be no surprise to my God. I will not fear tomorrow, for the Lord of Glory has preceded me into the future and prepared a way for me where there was no way.

"There shall no evil befall thee, neither shall any plague come nigh thy dwelling. For he shall give his angels charge over thee, to keep thee in all thy ways. They shall bear thee up in their hands, lest thou dash thy foot against a stone. Thou shalt tread upon the lion and adder: the young lion and the dragon shalt thou trample under feet. Because he hath set his love upon me, therefore will I deliver him: I will set him on high, because he hath known my name. He shall call upon me, and I will answer him: I will be with him in trouble; I will deliver him, and honour him" (Psalm 91:10-15).

I spit in the face of cancer.

I dance on the defeated head of discouragement, for I am the heritage of Jehovah, the Lord of Glory. "He is my Shepherd, you lying devil, and I am not some weak failure."

With the world falling apart around me, I am safe.

With AIDS sweeping the continent, I am safe.

With the economy falling apart, I am safe ... because I am sheltered within the arms of God.

He walks with me, He talks with me, and nothing on the face of this earth shall harm me. Greater is my God who is in me, in front of me, behind me, beside me, beneath me, above me, than the devil that is in the world.

"Ye are of God, little children, and have overcome them: because greater is he that is in you, than he that is in the world" (1 John 4:4).

Cheer up; dry those tears; stick out your chin. Go ahead and spit into the wind, for nothing on the face of this earth shall harm you.

I am not afraid of tomorrow.

If this hunk of clay falls over in the next thirty seconds, do not weep for me, because I will be seated in heavenly places. Carry on the vision and keep right on preaching. I will be cheering, for the last foe to be defeated in the arena of fear is the fear of death, and I am not afraid.

Deep down inside, if you are born again, you need not be afraid.

So why fear what the economy is going to do?

Why are you afraid of losing your job?

Why are you afraid things are falling apart around you?

Why are you afraid to walk down the street?

I want you to get a revelation of Jesus standing, battle-scarred, with His staff in one hand and the keys of the Kingdom in the other. He has been in conflict, and He is victorious!

Do not be afraid of tomorrow.

Do not be afraid of eternity, because He has already gone before you. Jesus is your way-maker.

You say, "Pastor Rod, my circumstances are so bad, I do not know if there is any way out."

Yes, there is! Jesus is a way-maker.

One day He made a way for me.

When my heart was dark and weary, Jesus came and answered my prayer. He brought me out of darkness and into light, out of death and into life, out of chains and into freedom.

He did it for me, and He will do it for you.

Hold Fast to His Word

"Oh, devil ... old boy, I know that you have no time for me and I guess you have about learned that I have no time for you. I will never apologize to you for anything I have done against you. If I have ever said anything that does not hurt you, tell me about it and I will take it out of my sermon.

"We thank thee, Jesus, for that manifestation of thy power in one of the big factories of the city. Lord, we are told that of eighty men who used to go to a saloon for their lunch, seventy-nine go there no more. All these men heard the 'booze' sermon. Lord, they are working on the one man who is standing out and they'll get him, too. The saloon-keeper is standing with arms akimbo behind the bar, but his old customers give the place the go-by. Thank you, Jesus."

- Billy Sunday

"But call to remembrance the former days, in which, after ye were illuminated, ye endured a great fight of afflictions" (Hebrews 10:32).

"Do you know what God is telling the body of Christ today? Take your dreams, your plans, your hopes, your aspirations, and the things you love the most and give them to me."
- Pastor Rod Parsley

God will champion the cause of His elect. He will bare His right arm to them that bow the knee to Him.

I want God to do something in me — to take tribulation and turn it into triumph so I can be a witness that greater is He that is in me than he that is in the world (1 John 4:4).

If we do not have something better than the world has, then we have nothing to preach about. I believe we do have something better than the world, and we should climb to the housetops and shout it aloud.

God spoke to Abraham and said, "I am going to make a great nation out of you."

"Now the Lord had said unto Abram, Get thee out of thy country, and from thy kindred, and from thy father's house, unto a land that I will shew thee: And I will make of thee a great nation, and I will bless thee, and make thy name great; and thou shalt be a blessing: And I will bless them that bless thee, and curse him that curseth thee: and in thee shall all families of the earth be blessed" (Genesis 12:1-3).

But Abraham tried to take things into his own hands, and the result was Ishmael.

God said, "He is not the one. You tried it your way, now try it mine."

The Bible says Sarah conceived and brought forth a child, and they called his name Isaac. Isaac grew up to be a young man much loved by his father. And every time his father saw him, he saw the promise of God and the fulfillment of his spiritual destiny. But do you know what God said to Abraham?

"Take now thy son, thine only son Isaac, whom thou lovest, and get thee into the land of Moriah; and offer him there for a burnt offering upon one of the mountains which I will tell thee of" (Genesis 22:2).

Do you know what God is telling the body of Christ today? "Take your dreams, your plans, your hopes, your aspirations — the things you love the most — and give them to me."

On the mountain, Abraham lifted up his hand to slay his son, and God stopped it in midair. He said, "I have seen your heart."

"And he said, Lay not thine hand upon the lad, neither do thou any thing unto him: for now I know that thou fearest God, seeing thou hast not withheld thy son, thine only son from me" (Genesis 22:12).

Only in death is there life: by dying to yourself and heeding THE WORD of God.

The way to live is to die.

The way to receive is to give.

The way to win is to surrender.

Abraham heard God's voice, and God stopped his hand.

Take your Bible and hold it in your hands. Open it up and leaf through its pages. The Book you hold in your hand is God's Word ... to you!

It is sacred and holy. Every word in it, from cover to cover, is divinely inspired. A solemn warning is given to those who would add to or take away from the words that are written in it.

"For I testify unto every man that heareth the words of the prophecy of this book, If any man shall add unto these things, God shall add unto him the plagues that are written in this book: And if any man shall take away from the words of the book of this prophecy, God shall take away his part out of the book of life, and out of the holy city, and from the things which are written in this book" (Revelation 22:18,19).

The Bible is God's voice to us.

God's Word is eternal. It has no beginning of days and it has no ending of life. When the earth was without form, and when darkness covered the earth, the Word was.

God's Word does not change. It is the same yesterday, today and forever.

Men change. Doctrines change. Ideals change. But the Word of God never changes!

In these perilous times, it is vital we know the purpose of the Word is to destroy the works of the devil.

"For this purpose the Son of God was manifested, that he might destroy the works of the devil" (1 John 3:8).

Abraham trusted the Word of God, and provided a sacrifice in the mountains.

Today, God is saying to us, "Now it is YOUR turn to make the sacrifice. Build yourself an altar. Climb up on that altar and lay down."

But you know what we do?

We try to provide the sacrifice every other way but in the mountain of God. We do not ever go to the mountain of God. We cannot make the sacrifice unless we get in the mountain, because the sacrifice is provided in the mountain.

Now look what happened decades later.

We find a man named David who had sinned, and because of his sin, a blight had come upon the entire nation of Israel. King David sat in sackcloth and ashes, and God said to him, "Go to Ornan's threshing floor."

"Then the angel of the Lord commanded Gad to say to David, that David should go up,

195

and set up an altar unto the Lord in the threshingfloor of Ornan the Jebusite" (1 Chronicles 21:18).

Ornan's threshing floor, decades later, was located on the same spot where Abraham had offered Isaac on Mount Moriah!

We try to offer sacrifices with our good works.

We go to church; we serve on the deacon board; we usher. We try to do all the good works.

God says, "Wait a minute. You are offering me a polluted sacrifice."

We must say, "Take my hopes, my dreams, my plans, and I will still worship You, because you are my God. I know the truth of your Word, Lord, and I will not be moved from its truth."

Having been illuminated by God's Word, I will not be deterred by the great fight of affliction.

We must purpose in our heart to refuse to cast away our confidence in God. We must not take matters into our own hands, lest we produce an Ishmael. Remember, Ishmael was circumcised in the same way Isaac was. In essence, he had the sign of the covenant, yet he (Ishmael) became a curse.

Trust the Word of God.

He will fulfill His Word to you.

The only help God needs from us is to move "self" out of the way. The only way to do that is to lay our flesh on the altar and become a living sacrifice.

Throughout the ages, men have tried to wipe out every trace of the Bible — the written Word — from the face of the earth. They have ridiculed it, spit on it, banned it from their country, burned it, tried to discredit it, called it myths and fairy tales. Men have twisted the Word of God and perverted it with their doctrines.

But, in spite of all these attacks, the Word still stands!

It has not lost its power.

From the very beginning, as the disciples began to speak forth the Word in the name of Jesus, Satan tried to stop them. The disciples were thrown in jail, beaten, and commanded not to speak or teach the Word.

It did not stop God's Word.

Satan could not stop the Word from going forth. Instead, the Word of God increased.

"So mightily grew the word of God and prevailed" (Acts 19:20).

Paul, who was bound and thrown into prison for preaching the Word, wrote to Timothy:

"Remember that Jesus Christ of the seed of David was raised from the dead according to my gospel: Wherein I suffer trouble, as an evil doer,

even unto bonds; but the word of God is not bound" (2 Timothy 2:8,9).

God and His Word are inseparable!

The Word has creative power.

It is unchangeable.

It is alive.

It cannot fail.

The Bible tells us perilous times will come and shake up the world in these last days. But God has not planned any defeats for us. As we fix our faith and trust in the Word of God, nothing can shake us.

God is preparing an endtime people who are so strong the devil will tremble in their presence, just as he trembled when Jesus addressed him.

No power of the enemy can defeat us as we fulfill the words of Jesus:

"If ye abide in me, and my words abide in you, ye shall ask what ye will, and it shall be done unto you" (John 15:7).

Remember, the SAME POWER that spoke the sun, moon, and stars into existence...

The SAME POWER that spoke forth the dry land, the forests, the mountains, and created the rivers and the oceans...

The SAME POWER that spoke into creation all the animals, the birds, the fish, and all forms of life...

The SAME POWER that spoke man into creation from the dust of the earth and breathed life into him...

The SAME POWER of the Word is in us!

The Word which in the beginning was God; the Word which was and is God; the Word which created all things — became flesh.

Now that Living Word dwells within us.

Avoid the Lap of Delilah

"There is many a life today which has no song. The most popular song for most of you would be:
'Where is that joy which once I knew,
When first I loved the Lord?'

"Right behind you where you left it when you went to that card party; right where you left it when you began to go to the theater; right where you left it when you side-stepped and backslid; right where you left it when you began paying one hundred dollars for a dress and gave twenty-five cents to the Lord; right where you left it when you began to gossip."

- Billy Sunday

"And she said, The Philistines be upon thee, Samson. And he awoke out of his sleep, and said, I will go out as at other times before, and shake myself. And he wist not that the Lord was departed from him" (Judges 16:20).

"You have been going where you should not go, seeing what you should not see, and hearing what you should not hear."

- Pastor Rod Parsley

What happened to Samson to cause the Lord to depart from him?

Samson went where he should not have gone.

"Then went Samson to Gaza, and saw there an harlot, and went in unto her" (Judges 16:1).

He went where he should not have gone, and he saw what he should not have seen.

When we go where we should not go, we are going to see what we should not see. When we go where we should not go, we are going to hear what we should not hear. When we go where we should not go, we are going to do what we should not do.

No one forced Samson to go; he went because he wanted to go. Do not ever let anyone, including the lying devil, dupe you with the pretense he made you or forced you into doing anything sinful.

The devil did not cause most of the trouble we go through.

Most of the time, we cause our own problems.

As blood-bought, Holy Ghost filled, fire baptized believers, we have no one to blame for our problems but ourselves. We have been going where we should not go, seeing what we should not see, hearing what we should not hear, and doing what we should not do.

"And it was told the Gazites, saying, Samson is come hither. And they compassed him in, and laid wait for him all night in the gate of the city, and were quiet all the night, saying, In the morning when it is day, we shall kill him. And Samson lay till midnight, and arose at midnight, and took the doors of the gate of the city, and the two posts, and went away with them, bar and all, and put them upon his shoulders, and carried them up to the top of an hill that is before Hebron" (Judges 16:2,3).

In this passage, Samson still had some power left!

He was going where he should not go, but he still had power.

He was seeing what he should not see, but he still had power.

He was hearing what he should not hear, but he still had power.

He was doing what he should not do, but his power was still there.

I imagine Samson repented all the way home, but the devil is relentless. He wants ALL the power we have.

Delilah, the devil's agent, wanted to take all Samson's power, so she asked him, *"Tell me, I pray thee, wherein thy great strength lieth, and wherewith thou mightest be bound to afflict thee"* *(Judges 16:6).*

At first, Samson lied and told her to bind him with *"seven green whips that were never dried" (v.7).* When that failed, he told her to bind him with *"new ropes that never were occupied" (v.11).* But that failed. A third time she asked, and Samson told her to *"weave the seven locks of my head with the web" (v.13).*

That too failed, but Delilah was relentless. She *"pressed him daily with her words, and urged him, so that his soul was vexed unto death" (v.16).*

As long as you live in the devil's territory — in the lap of Delilah — the devil will never give up on you until he has you.

Finally, Samson gave up and told Delilah what she wanted to know: *"If I be shaven [on his head], then my strength will go from me, and I shall become weak, and be like any other man" (v.17).*

God made His power available to Samson, but he ultimately lost that power living in the lap of sin.

God has also given us His power. The Bible says, to as many as would receive Him, to them He gave power.

"But as many as received him, to them gave he power to become the sons of God, even to them that believe on his name" (John 1:12).

Now, either He gave us power, or He is a liar. And if God is a liar, we should all throw our Bibles in a big bonfire. If we cannot have the power God said was available to us, then God is a liar.

God is not a liar!

"God forbid: yea, let God be true, but every man a liar; as it is written, That thou mightest be justified in thy sayings, and mightest overcome when thou art judged" (Romans 3:4).

His power is available to as many as receive Jesus — and stay out of the lap of sin.

He gave you and me the power to defeat the enemy!

When?

When we received Him.

That power is not exclusive; it is available to all mankind."

The Lord is not slack concerning his promise, as some men count slackness; but is longsuffering to us-ward, not willing that any should perish, but that all should come to repentance" (2 Peter 3:9).

Only when Samson left the lap of Delilah and repented of his sin did God restore his strength.

"And Samson called unto the Lord, and said, O Lord God, remember me, I pray thee, and strengthen me, I pray thee, only this once, O God, that I may be at once avenged of the Philistines for my two eyes" (Judges 16:8).

Today, if you are living in the lap of Delilah, get out while you still have the strength! Don't let the devil steal your power.

Don't Quit

"Commodore Vanderbilt had a fortune of over $200,000,000, and one day when he was ill he sent for Dr. Deems. He asked him to sing for him that old song:

'Come, ye sinners, poor and needy,
"Come, ye wounded, sick and sore.'

"The old Commodore tossed from side to side, looked around at the evidence of his wealth, and said: 'That is what I am, poor and needy.'

"Who? Commodore Vanderbilt poor and needy with his $200,000,000? The foundation of that fabulous fortune was laid by him when he poled a yawl from New York to Staten Island and picked up pennies for doing it.

"The foundation of the immense Astor fortune was laid by John Jacob Astor when he went out and bought fur and hides from trappers and put the money in New York real estate.

"The next day on the street, one man said to another: 'Have you heard the news? Commodore Vanderbilt is dead.' 'How much did he leave?,' the other asked. The first man replied, 'He left nothing at all.'

"Naked you came into this world, and naked you will crawl out of it. You brought nothing into the world, and you will take nothing out. And if you have put the pack screws on the poor and piled up a pile of gold as big as a house, you cannot take it with you. It wouldn't do you any good if you could, because it would melt."

- Billy Sunday in The Man and His Message

"Nay, in all these things we are more than conquerors through him that loved us" (Romans 8:37).

"Stay faithful to God. Never quit — never allow bitterness or anger to set in your spirit — and your life will become a living temple to glorify His holy name."

- Pastor Rod Parsley

From the time he was seventeen, God gave Joseph, the son of Jacob, the ability to interpret the meaning of dreams. Joseph was a faithful and godly man who was loved dearly by his father — so much so his own brothers despised and hated him.

"And when his brethren saw that their father loved him more than all his brethren, they hated him, and could not speak peaceably unto him" (Genesis 37:4).

So deep was the jealousy of Joseph's brothers they *"conspired against him to slay him" (Genesis 37:18).* Finally, instead of killing him, they decided to cast young Joseph into a deep pit.

Joseph was soon taken out of the deep pit and sold into slavery to Midianite merchantmen for twenty pieces of silver. These merchants then brought Joseph into Egypt where they sold him to Potiphar, an officer of Pharaoh and the captain of the guard.

Throughout all these undeserved events, there is nothing written anywhere in the Bible to indicate Joseph ever said, "God, I have served you faithfully. I love you. So why are you doing these things to me?"

Joseph never quit in His service and love of the Lord. Joseph never uttered one negative word against God. He trusted God, and remained faithful despite the perilous times in his own life.

He never quit.

He never blamed God for his problems!

When Joseph was brought into Egypt, so strong was his relationship with God the circumstances the devil intended for evil were turned around for good.

"The Lord was with Joseph, and he was a prosperous man; and he was in the house of his master the Egyptian" (Genesis 39:2).

So faithful was Joseph to God even his heathen master took note of his love of the Lord.

"And his master saw that the Lord was with him, and that the Lord made all that he did to prosper in his hand" (Genesis 39:3).

The enemy was not going to stand to see Joseph prosper, so the devil used Potiphar's wife as an instrument to destroy Joseph. She *"cast her eyes upon Joseph; and she said, Lie with me"* (Genesis 39:7).

Joseph refused, saying *"How then can I do this great wickedness, and sin against God?"* (Genesis 39:9).

But Potiphar's wife would not be deterred. Like the devil, she was persistent to achieve her wicked end.

Again Joseph refused, this time fleeing while she tugged at his garment, ripping it off of him (Genesis 39:13).

Potiphar's wife was so angry at Joseph's rejection she lied to her husband, claiming Joseph had entered her room and tried to sleep with her, leaving his garment behind as he fled from the bedroom while she cried out in protest.

As a result of his wife's false accusations, Potiphar tossed Joseph into prison.

But Joseph STILL did not quit on God!

He continued to be a godly man — even though his brothers had rejected him, even though he had been thrown into a pit, even though he had been sold into slavery, and now, even though he was thrown into prison for something he did not do!

Because Joseph kept his eyes focused on God, *"the Lord was with Joseph, and shewed him mercy, and gave him favour in the sight of the keeper of the prison" (Genesis 39:19).*

Do you see the pattern here?

God was taking things meant for evil and was converting them into events to be used for good.

Why?

Because Joseph remained faithful.

Despite perilous circumstances, he never once quit on God!

His brothers sold Joseph into slavery — yet Joseph became the head of a rich household in Egypt.

Potiphar's wife lied about Joseph and sent him to prison — yet in prison, he prospered *"because the Lord was with him, and that which he did, the Lord made it to prosper" (Genesis 39:23).*

While in prison, Joseph interpreted dreams for Potiphar's butler and baker, and both dreams came to pass. Despite the chief butler's promise to remember Joseph, he *"forgat him."*

Once again, Joseph could have become bitter at the chief butler's broken promise, and quit on God. For two more years, Joseph remained in jail.

Abandoned.

He could have become bitter then.

He could have been angry with God.

But Joseph remained faithful, refusing to quit on God, no matter how bad his current circumstances seemed.

TWO YEARS LATER — the Pharaoh had dreams. No magician or wise man in Egypt could *"interpret them unto Pharaoh" (Genesis 41:8).*

TWO YEARS LATER — the chief butler finally remembered how Joseph had correctly interpreted his dream, and told the Pharaoh about him.

TWO YEARS LATER — Joseph could have become bitter and sarcastic. He could have spent those two years cursing God because of the time he had to spend in prison.

But Joseph did not quit on God.

He trusted Him.

When Pharaoh sent for Joseph to interpret his dreams, Joseph humbly stated, *"It is not in me: God shall give Pharaoh an answer of peace" (Genesis 41:16).* After two years, Joseph was still serving God — he did not quit!

God gave Joseph the ability to interpret the dreams, and he warned that Egypt would have seven good years for harvest, followed by seven years of famine. Joseph devised a plan to store wheat during times of plenty so Egypt would be prepared for the time of famine. Pharaoh appointed Joseph in charge of the project, saying *"only in the throne will I be greater than thou" (Genesis 41:40).*

Because Joseph did not quit on God during his times of peril, God continually gave him favor, and eventually — like Job — blessed the latter end of his life even more than the former.

You know the rest of the story. Joseph eventually sold wheat to his brothers — the very men who sold him into slavery! Joseph's brothers were sure he would kill them when their father Jacob died, but Joseph reassured them, *"Fear not: for am I in the place of God? But as for you, ye thought evil against me; but God meant it unto good ... I will nourish you, and your little ones. And he comforted them, and spake kindly unto them" (Genesis 50:19-21).*

These are the actions of a man unmoved by his circumstances — a man who never gave up on God during the toughest of times.

He proclaimed ... "What was meant for evil God has converted to good."

He proclaimed ... "I will not kill you. Instead, I will nourish you — and your children."

Joseph died at one hundred and ten years old, a godly man who refused to quit through the most perilous and frustrating of times.

When he was sold into slavery — he did not quit.

When he was falsely accused and imprisoned — he did not quit.

When he was forgotten — he did not quit.

The devil's strategy for your life is to make you quit. He will bring trouble into your life, hoping in your desperation you will accuse God as the source of your trouble ... and quit.

The devil hopes to wear you down through frustration, anger and desperation, until finally you give up on God.

God NEVER gives up on you.

Follow Joseph's example.

Stay faithful to God when trouble comes. Never doubt God because of your circumstances. He will always lead you out.

Stay faithful to God.

Never quit.

Never allow bitterness or anger to settle in your spirit and rob you of the blessings God intends for you.

Like Joseph, in every situation — good or bad — let your life become a living temple to glorify His holy name.

"You do not have the Spirit of a quitter living inside you; you have the Spirit of the only man in history to conquer death. You have the Spirit of a winner — the Spirit of Jesus Christ inside you."

- Pastor Rod Parsley

Jesus walked, blood-soaked, beaten, and battered on that rough and rocky road to Calvary — kicked and prodded through the dirty streets of Jerusalem. If He were ever going to quit, that would have been the time for Him to do it.

But when Judas betrayed him with a kiss, Jesus did not turn from God.

When Peter denied Him three times, He did not turn from God.

When Pilate washed his hands of this innocent man, He did not turn from God.

When the skin on his back was viciously ripped away by a whip, when a mock crown of sharp thorns punctured his brow, He did not turn from God.

When huge spikes were driven into His hands and feet, He did not turn from God.

Three days after His death, Jesus broke the bondage of the grave and rose from the dead, declaring loudly to the world, "I am the Christ, the Son of the Living God, and not even death can turn me from God."

Today, that same victorious Christ who overcomes ALL perilous circumstances lives inside you.

You do not have the Spirit of a quitter living inside you; you have the Spirit of the only man in history ever to conquer death.

You have the Spirit of a winner — the Spirit of Jesus Christ living inside you.

And YOU are not going to quit.

As you read this book, you may feel like giving up. You may feel like the crushing circumstances of your deteriorating marriage are too much to bear.

You may feel like your monthly bills have become so huge and so hopeless there is no way out.

You may be convinced your unsaved child is so firmly rooted in addiction nothing will ever make a difference.

I have news for you.

You are a child of God, and God does not quit!

Take your eyes off your circumstances. Like Joseph, do not look at the confines of your prison walls; see the magnitude of your God.

Do not look at the depth of the pit you are in; recognize the power of God to lead you out!

Do not look at the false accusations of others and say, "Woe is me." Instead, praise God for His protection as He brings you through the fire.

You are not going to quit because greater is He that is in you that he that is in the world.

When you give your life to Him, when you die to yourself, He resurrects you into His glory.

God will never quit on you.

Remember, gauge your success or failure only by God's yardstick. Even in prison, Joseph was a success in God's eyes because he remained faithful to God.

Joseph had many ups and downs, but he decided to use his seeming failures as opportunities ... and in the end he was victorious!

Reflect the Christ Life

My Father's Business

"Be out and out for God. Have a heart-to-heart talk with some people and win them to Christ. The first recorded words of Jesus are these: "Wist ye not that I must be about my Father's business?"

"The trouble is we are too lackadaisical in religion, indifferent, dead and lifeless. That is the spirit of the committees today in the church. I think the multitude in the church will have to get converted themselves before they can lead anyone else to Christ. It is my firm conviction, after many years of experience in the work, that half the people in the church have never been converted, have never been born again.

"I take up a bottle of water, uncork it and take a drink. That is experimental. One sip of water can convince me more of water's power to satisfy thirst than 40,000 books written on the subject.

"You know quinine water is bitter because you have experimented; you know fire will burn because you have experimented; you know ice will freeze your hands because you have experimented.

"A man must experience religion to know God."

- Billy Sunday, the Man and His Message.

"The youngest babe in Christ is much more than a match for the devil."
- Pastor Rod Parsley

One thing is certain, light will always dispel darkness. No night was ever so deep dawn could not dispel it.

"For whatsoever is born of God overcometh the world: and this is the victory that overcometh the world, even our faith" (1 John 5:4).

You do not overcome darkness because of what you have done, you overcome darkness because of who you are in Christ.

I have two small children at home. As long as I can breathe and move, they will always overcome hunger. They are born of the Parsley family, and they will overcome whatever Rod Parsley can overcome.

My wife and two children will be nurtured and protected by me because of who they are — members of my family. As long as I can stand, no one is ever going to hurt them, and they are never going to go hungry!

You are a member of God's family.

God lovingly stands over you, around you, and lives personally within you. As long as you belong to God's family, no enemy is ever going to hurt you, and you are never going to go hungry or unprotected.

"The thief cometh not, but for to steal, and to kill, and to destroy: I am come that they might have life, and that they might have it more abundantly" (John 10:10).

You are in the family of Christ, and God wants to take care of you and give you abundant life.

Now, let me be very frank here. I have heard many preachers use John 10:10 as a sermon text to claim God wants us to totally prosper in all areas all the time!

That is not the case if you view prosperity and abundance through the world's eyes.

Joseph enjoyed God's abundance while he was in prison because he knew whom he served, and served Him with a glad heart.

Abundant life in God's eyes does not mean everything that discomforts your flesh is of the devil, and everything that comforts your flesh is of God.

It means we participate in the nature and the life of Christ, and we are abundant in all circumstances — even though they may be perilous!

Joseph enjoyed God's abundance because he knew the nature of God, and rejoiced in the privilege of being able to serve HIM.

In the family of God, we rejoice with Jesus Christ as we share in His suffering, and we rejoice when we share His resurrection from the dead.

The true representation of your character is not how you respond on the mountaintop; but like Joseph, how you respond in prison — how you respond to the raging fires and floods of life.

Television has become the medium that dictates its false, perverted values and morals to America.

But television does not reflect Christ.

To be more like Christ, you must go to another source — the Word of God!

Let the Word be the mirror of what the Christ life is to you.

You say, "I want to live a full live."

Jesus replies, "If you want to live, know that this is not a fantasy world. If you want to live, then you first must die. Die to yourself. Die to your will. Die to your way, and let my Christlikeness be produced in you."

That is the only way.

"Do not see how close you can come to the world and still be in Christ. Rather, see how close you can get to God and still be in this world."

- Pastor Rod Parsley

Scripture constantly warns us to be careful to avoid evil, and places where evil abounds.

"Abstain from all appearance of evil" (1 Thessalonians 5:22).

Stay away from the miry places (Ezekiel 47:1-5).

"He brought me through the waters; the waters were to the ancles" (Ezekiel 47:3).

Along the bank of the river of God's will is the place where water and land meet. You would be better to stay on dry terra firma than to stir around in the mud of the shallows.

God despises those who are lukewarm.

"I know thy works, that thou art neither cold nor hot: I would thou wert cold or hot. So then because thou art lukewarm, and neither cold nor hot, I will spue thee out of my mouth" (Revelation 3:15,16).

Little Johnnie fell out of bed in the night. His mother asked him why he fell. Johnnie responded, "I stayed too close to where I got in at."

Do not try to see how close you can come to the world and still be in Christ. Rather, see how close you can draw to God and still function in this world. Satan's works will be destroyed as you manifest Jesus in your life. Manifest Christlikeness in both the good times and the bad, with those who are loveable and those who are unloveable.

Be like Jesus in every area of your life.

When Jesus was persecuted, He asked His Heavenly Father to forgive His accusers, and to release of any guilt those who drove the nails into His hands.

Let Christ's life come out in you — THAT is what destroys the works of the enemy.

"He that committeth sin is of the devil; for the devil sinneth from the beginning. For this purpose the Son of God was manifested, that he might destroy the works of the devil" (1 John 3:8).

Christ in you will annihilate the works of the devil.

David prayed, *"Keep back thy servant also from presumptuous sins; let them not have dominion over me: then shall I be upright, and I shall be innocent from the great transgression" (Psalm 19:13).*

He was saying, "Lord deliver me from the idolatrous sin of presumption that I would think you are something you are not."

Manifesting Christlikeness means manifesting who Christ is — in you.

It means manifesting humility.

It means forgiving the unforgivable, and loving those who do not deserve your love.

It means being willing to give up something temporal to gain something eternal.

Because of your Christlikeness, because you are born of God, you can overcome anything God can. The youngest babe in Christ is more than a match for the devil.

"Nay, in all these things we are more than conquerors through him that loved us" (Roman 8:37).

CONCLUSION

Troubled Times, Supernatural Strength

You and I are in the final moments of endtime spiritual history. This IS the perilous, troubled time (2 Timothy 3:1)!

But while the world is crumbling in moral and financial chaos, you do not need to be troubled.

By implementing these survival strategies in this book, you now have hope beyond the troubled times of endtime humanity!

As a spirit man, you are not dictated to and dominated by human limitations. You can rise above the seen into the unseen (2 Corinthians 4:18).

Armed with these strategies, you can face all temptation, conquer cancer, cast off enemy attack, and overcome any financial obstacle ... in HIS supernatural strength!

The world is not going to get better; it is going to get worse. But as you put these twenty strategies to work, you will have the supernatural strength and power of God protecting and covering you in the midst of troubled times.

He will meet your every need!

You may be facing the greatest trials and conflicts of your life — but you are not facing them alone!

He will meet your every need!

Yes, God is shaking this world (Hebrews 12:26,27), but through making these survival strategies a part of your daily walk, you will emerge victorious!

Do not let your natural circumstances dictate your spiritual altitude. Remember, Jesus went into the grave and came out victorious on the other side. He set the pattern.

You are His child, and He has given you the same supernatural strength to overcome every circumstance in your life.

Lift up your eyes!

Angels are surrounding you!

The blood of Jesus is covering you (Hebrews 2:14)!

You are born into a supernatural Kingdom that cannot be moved. It is only when you step outside the Kingdom of God that you have anything to fear in this world.

God will preserve you in the midst of trouble.

In the last days, God promises to pour out His Spirit on all flesh (Acts 2:17-19). God is turning up the heat, but you will be swimming in the cool pool of the living water of the Holy Spirit!

Remember, it does not matter what circumstances you are facing today, or what circumstances you will encounter tomorrow. If you will apply God's survival strategies to your life, you will have the supernatural strength to be victorious in EVERY circumstance!